LOUIS RORIMER

Louis Rorimer, 1872–1939. *Courtesy of the Rorimer family.*

LOUIS RORIMER
A Man of Style

Leslie A. Piña

THE KENT STATE UNIVERSITY PRESS
Kent, Ohio, and London, England

© 1990 by The Kent State University Press, Kent, Ohio 44242
All rights reserved
Library of Congress Catalog Card Number 90–34121
ISBN 0–87338–418–0
Manufactured in the United States of America

Library of Congress Cataloging-in-Publication Data

Piña, Leslie A., 1947–
    Louis Rorimer : a man of style / Leslie A. Piña.
        p. cm.
    Includes bibliographical references.
    ISBN 0–87338–418–0 (alk. paper) ∞
    1. Rorimer, Louis, 1872–1939—Criticism and interpretation.
2. Interior decorators—United States—Biography. 3. Rorimer-
Brooks Studios. 4. Decorative arts—United States—History—20th
century.   I. Title.
NK2004.3.R67P5   1990
729'.092—dc20   90–34121
                                                                    CIP

British Library Cataloging-in-Publication data are available.

CONTENTS

CHRONOLOGY

1872 Louis Rorimer born Sept. 12, Cleveland, Ohio

1890–95 Rorimer studies art in Europe

1896–98 Rohrheimer and Bowman Studio, 442 Old Arcade

1898–1904 Rohrheimer and Hays, studios 901–5 Garfield Building, workshops 154–58 Champlain Street

1904–05 Rohrheimer Studios, 277–85 Old Erie Street near Euclid Avenue

1906–10 Rorheimer Studios, 1907–31 East Ninth Street

1910–16 Rorheimer-Brooks Studios, 1907–31 East Ninth Street

1916–39 Rorimer-Brooks Studios, 2232 Euclid Avenue

1939 Rorimer dies Nov. 30

1939–57 Rorimer-Brooks, Inc., 2232 Euclid Avenue

INTRODUCTION

In 1892, while studying art in Munich, young Louis Rorimer wrote to his brother-in-law in Cleveland to ask for money to go to Paris. "I believe in ones going to the best place if he can," Rorimer wrote. For the next half century Rorimer's knack for recognizing opportune places was a key element in the making of an American success story. He was a gifted designer among many other talented artists, yet Rorimer was unique in the ability to realize his artistic, economic, and personal dreams.

Five years studying, making contacts, and witnessing the exciting events taking place on the European art scene of the 1890s established Europe as Rorimer's source of ideas on the international level, and throughout his lifetime he returned there on a regular basis. New York was the major link between Rorimer-Brooks and the national scene, and Rorimer commuted even more frequently to New York. Although he chose his birthplace, Cleveland, Ohio, as the location for his interior design studios, his reputation soon spread and Rorimer-Brooks Studios became one of America's leading interior design firms.[1]

Whereas Europe and New York provided cultural enrichment and contacts, Cleveland offered great economic opportunities in the early twentieth century. Industrial and commercial growth begat residential expansion, particularly in the suburbs, and the eastern suburbs became Rorimer's most reliable market. Increased prosperity and awareness of a need for professional interior designers provided the climate in which Rorimer-Brooks flourished. There was considerable need yet few sources for high-quality interior design in the Cleveland area, and Rorimer had the good fortune and the good sense to remain there in the midst of its development.

Except for a short-lived branch studio at Shaker Square, Cleveland's exclusive suburban shopping area, Rorimer-Brooks's only location was in downtown Cleveland. Rorimer built the first commercial building on "Millionaires' Row," at 2232 Euclid Avenue through Studios Realty Company, of which he was president. The Northern Italian classical-style building was selected from among 180 commercial buildings of three or less stories erected in Cleveland in 1916

1

Rorimer-Brooks Studios in a Northern Italian classical-style building at 2232 Euclid Avenue, built in 1916 and awarded a medal by the Cleveland Chamber of Commerce. *Courtesy of the Press Collection, Cleveland State University.*

and awarded a medal by the Cleveland Chamber of Commerce in 1917. Meade and Hamilton were the architects and Christian, Schwartzberg and Gaede were the engineers.[2] Rorimer's building housed a gallery-like studio and all of the workshops needed to produce primarily handcrafted and custom-designed furnishings. There were no facilities for mass production, which limited the production capability of the studio's hundred or more employees. What Rorimer-Brooks did not manufacture it acquired from numerous American and foreign companies for subsequent resale. Their inventory included the best imported antiques and hand-blocked wallpapers available (both of which Rorimer-Brooks became known for), as well as standard decorating items such as carpets, fabrics, lamps, and pictures. Occasionally a Rorimer-Brooks design was produced, or even mass-produced, by other companies. Rorimer's success was due to his ability to manufacture or acquire unusual items in addition to the finest traditional goods. The range of styles was broad, but there was no room for variation in quality. Rorimer-Brooks's consistent reputation for high

2

standards can be attributed to Rorimer's close personal supervision and a clientele willing to pay his price.

Even during the Great Depression, the company was able to maintain the same quality it had enjoyed earlier, although cutbacks in staff and production were sometimes necessary. Long before 1939, when Rorimer died, he had won a national reputation for the Statler Hotel chain interiors, as well as for being a midwestern tastemaker. Although the company continued to operate until 1957, its most important years were those under Rorimer's direction. These were also some of the most fertile years for American design, particularly the 1920s and 1930s. These decades witnessed the advent of modernism in American design, a modernism which even broke from European forms, the source of American design for three centuries. Rorimer's participation and leadership in the development of American modernism were initially tied to European events.

His first venture into a modern style was connected to the Arts and Crafts movement. Examples of Rorimer's Arts and Crafts pieces from the beginning of the twentieth century can be compared to designs by his American and European contemporaries who achieved international acclaim. Modern styles of Arts and Crafts and later Art Deco were but two of many modes that Rorimer worked in, because he was not only a designer of furniture, but of complete interiors. His allegiance was to a wealthy and largely conservative population of homeowners and businessmen who desired Old World elegance in their personal environments. Rorimer's knowledge and love of antiques enabled him to serve his public well—so well that it was necessary to construct copies in order to satisfy the increasing demand for these historic styles. Because Rorimer-Brooks reached a balance between serving upper-middle-class taste and directing it, antiques and antique reproduction furniture became a specialty and a staple product of the company.

Rorimer's fluency in both traditional and modern idioms characterized his contribution to twentieth-century American interior design. The compatibility between traditional and modern design elements was something Rorimer believed in, and his work demonstrates that a designer can select one without rejecting the other. Because quality is timeless, Rorimer's design repertoire embraced the past, the present, and perhaps a bit of the future.

❧ 1 ❧

FOUNDATIONS

Louis Rorimer's parents, Jacob and Minnie Iglauer Rohrheimer,[1] emigrated to America from Lorsch in Hesse Darmstadt, Germany, in 1847. They arrived in Cleveland, Ohio, in 1849, where Jacob established a tobacco business that supported his family for the next forty years. Many German immigrants made cigars in Cleveland, and by 1880 a news report listed twenty-seven such firms. In the 1850s Jacob began by making cigars in his home on Pittsburgh Street in Cleveland. By the 1860s he had separate business addresses, always on or near Public Square, where he continued to manufacture and sell cigars. His brother Bernhard immigrated directly to Cleveland in 1853 and joined Jacob to form the J and B Rohrheimer Tobacco Company in the 1870s. It lasted until 1888, when Jacob retired and Bernhard changed the name of their business to B. Rohrheimer and Sons.[2]

In addition to his role as one of Cleveland's early business proprietors, Jacob Rohrheimer was active in the Jewish community, which had been founded by fellow Bavarian immigrants. He was one of the first Jewish settlers in Cleveland out of a total population of about 17,000 in 1850. From 1873 to 1874 Rohrheimer was treasurer of the Jewish Orphan Asylum, and from 1874 to 1884 he was president of Rabbi A. Hahn's congregation, Teffereth Israel, which would later become The Temple. Tefereth Israel, founded in 1850, was the first Reform Jewish congregation in Cleveland.[3]

Jacob and Minnie had seven children. The youngest, born on September 12, 1872, was named Louis, and from the age of four while he was learning to use words he was already expressing himself with crayons. As an artistically talented youngster, Louis was encouraged by his parents, who sent him to the very progressive Cleveland Manual Training School for his elementary education. The school was founded by Newton M. Anderson, who believed that a young man's training should include joining and carving wood, modeling clay, and forging iron as well as the traditional subjects—the classics, history, literature, and mathematics.[4] The school flourished under Anderson, who later founded University School. One of the instructors, the German-trained sculptor Herman Matzen, played an important part in the young Rorimer's life, both at the Manual Training School, where he taught modeling and carving, and later at the Cleveland School of Art.

By age fourteen, Rorimer showed promise as an artist and began taking courses at the Cleveland School of Art in its early headquarters, the old City Hall. As a growing industrial city in the late nineteenth century, Cleveland had relatively little to offer a talented young artist. Europe was the place to be, for the fortunate few who could afford it, and Rorimer was determined to go there. By 1890 his parents gave in to his dream, and he sailed for Europe, but in February 1891, shortly after Louis left, his father Jacob died. With the financial help of his brother-in-law Abe Stearn, Rorimer studied in Munich under professors Wideman and Romeis at the Kunstgewerbeschule, one of Europe's finest arts and crafts schools. Sharing its ideals with the Arts and Crafts movement, the Kunstgewerbeschule combined the teaching of design with craftsmanship, and no distinction was made between fine art and craft. He chose Munich because of his German background and language fluency and because Munich had been an attraction for hundreds of American artists seeking a European education, many of whom went on to become famous painters.[5]

Cleveland's art scene in the late nineteenth century was dominated by Germans and sons of German immigrants, and an important group of artists called themselves the Old Bohemians. Most of the members of the group had studied abroad in Munich, Paris, or London. Louis Loeb, one of the original members of the Old Bohemians, became a close friend of Rorimer's while he was studying in Europe.[6]

Rorimer wrote to Abe Stearn from Munich in July of 1892: "I have always heard so much of the taste of the French and that they turned out the best work and it naturally made me feel as if there was a better place to study than Munich. . . . [T]he saying is no wish no gain."[7] Rorimer's first year in Munich, including the fare from Cleveland, had cost almost $400, so he asked for $500 for one year in Paris, a costlier place to live. Rorimer also mentioned his plans to go to Berlin, Dresden, and other German cities with a fellow American artist, William Dietz.

Stearn provided the money, and in 1893 Rorimer studied in Paris at L'Ecole des Arts Décoratifs and at the Academie Julian. The Academie Julian was founded in 1868 by a minor painter and former wrestler, Rodolphe Julian. By the late 1880s the Academie was the most popular private art school in Paris, especially with foreigners who could not or would not attend the official government school, L'Ecole des Beaux-Arts. The Academie offered students the freedom to do a good deal of independent and unsupervised work.

Robert Henri studied at the Academie just prior to Rorimer's enrollment.[8] It is not likely that Rorimer met Henri at the Academie, but the two artists may have crossed paths in the early 1900s in New York, where Henri painted and taught and Rorimer visited. In 1910 the Exhibition of Independent Artists was a milestone in the history of modern art in America and a high point in

Rorimer (front center holding sausage) with William Dietz and friends in the Bavarian Alps in the 1890s. *Courtesy of the Rorimer family.*

Henri's career. Rorimer probably saw the exhibit, and early in 1911 seven of "the most progressive painters of Greater Cleveland"—Henry Keller, Gustav Hugger, Abel Warshawsky, Caroline Osborne, William Sommer, Carl Mollman, and Rorimer—called themselves "the Secessionists" and joined to follow the teachings of Henri. Rorimer's interior design studio served as a meeting place for the Secessionists as well as for other artist groups.[9] He also put his studio at the disposal of individual artists who found turn-of-the-century Cleveland to be an artistic vacuum.

In 1910 when Impressionist painter Abel Warshawsky returned home with the work he had done in Europe, he received a cool reception from Clevelanders, who regarded his paintings as crude and anarchistic. Although Rorimer admitted that "Paris was still a long way off from Cleveland," he was the only one to show interest in Warshawsky's paintings. Rorimer warned him that compared to the "dark brown school of painting" Warshawsky's work would appear like a pyrotechnical display. Still he provided a large gallery of his studios for a one-man show. Rorimer removed all of the artwork from the walls and arranged the showroom furnishings and lighting to show off Warshawsky's paintings and to provide an intimate viewing atmosphere. The show was well attended thanks to Rorimer's friends and some local artists and art lovers.[10]

Rorimer's European education had extended from the classroom to the cafés of Paris, where he mingled with figures in the forefront of contemporary artistic movements. After his first exposure to modern art in Paris in 1893, Rorimer was never again satisfied just to be a traditionalist. The 1890s were some of the most thrilling times to be an artist in Europe in the midst of the French Impressionist and Post-Impressionist movements, the British Aesthetic and Arts and Crafts movements, Symbolism, and Art Nouveau. Theories, styles, and artists crossed over the lines between movements, and an artist involved in any European art scene was exposed to a sea of ideas.

The roots of both the Aesthetic and the Arts and Crafts movements lay in reactions to the adverse effect industrialization had on art, as reflected in the Crystal Palace Exhibition of 1851. It was feared by reformers that the kinds of machine-made objects seen at the exhibition would destroy aesthetic standards and lead to the debasement of English taste. Mid-century demonstrations against the prevailing taste for inferior-quality goods inspired a movement that continued into the next century and changed its appearance as it crossed national boundaries. The English Arts and Crafts movement was spearheaded by John Ruskin, the art critic who sought design reform because he thought beauty and quality had been compromised for profit and quantity.[11]

William Morris practiced what Ruskin preached—joining art and labor and producing aesthetically pleasing and well-made goods. The William Morris workshops had been founded under the name of Morris, Morris, Faulkner, and Company in 1861 and were reorganized in 1875 as Morris and Company with William Morris as the only proprietor. The early furniture designs were by Ford Madox Brown and American-born Philip Webb, whose style influenced many British craft revival designers of the 1880s and 1890s.[12]

Morris and Company products and Morris's written ideas were easily accessible in England and in the United States. Morris also inspired emulation through his personal contacts with most English and some American figures connected with the Arts and Crafts movement. With the exception of the art pottery industry beginning in 1880, most American involvement in the movement took place after Morris's death in 1896, so only the earliest participants could have personally met Morris. Morris and Company remained in business until 1940. A William Morris Society was founded in Chicago in 1903, one of many Arts and Crafts societies popular in the United States around the turn of the century. Morris's designs were available in America in stores such as Marshall Field and Company and the Tobey Furniture Company in Chicago. Although Chicago was considered to be the most important regional focus of the Arts and Crafts movement, Cleveland was also an active midwestern center.[13] Rorimer was a (if not the) major Cleveland participant in the movement.

Morris was primarily a patternist, a prolific designer of wallpapers, fabrics, and other patterned designs. Ironically, he sold these to an upper-middle-class clientele because the high cost of manufacturing quality goods inevitably made them expensive. No doubt this frustrated a man who advocated socialism and disapproved of art for the few.

Rorimer, on the other hand, was comfortably capitalistic and was grateful for the steady stream of wealthy clients in the Midwest. This seems to be the only significant difference between his and Morris's artistic philosophies. Both were ardent supporters of quality—quality of design, of workmanship, and of the lives of the workers. Morris had looked back to both medieval design inspiration and the medieval organizations of craftsmen. Rorimer also had a taste for Gothic motifs, which he used freely, especially in carving.

One of the most controversial issues was over the use of machinery in producing previously handcrafted items. On the one hand, the Industrial Revolution was held responsible for the proliferation of mass-produced shoddy goods found in Victorian society and inspired those with any aesthetic sensibility to call for reform. Yet, according to Oscar Triggs, an Arts and Crafts leader and the founder of the Industrial Art League of Chicago in 1899, the machine had at least two positive effects on art. First, by turning out goods in such quantity, it created a need, or at least a demand, for art objects. What was then needed was an enlightened public that required tasteful objects rather than kitsch. Second, the machine could achieve only what it was programmed to do. If used wisely, it could do the dirty work—the boring, perhaps dangerous operations—and free men and women to enjoy more creative and satisfying jobs. Misuse of the machine for commercial gain was a temptation not easily resisted.[14]

The craftsman's place in society had been challenged by the Industrial Revolution. Craftsmen who had embodied both artist and workman were the unsuspecting victims of a machine age in which "cheap and nasty" goods abounded. What was called for by reformers such as Ruskin and Morris was a return to crafts and to craftsmanship by revitalizing art and elevating labor. According to Triggs, the return had to be within the new context of industrialization if it was to be anything more than an episode of nostalgia.

In a paper presented in 1925 at a convention of the American Federation of Arts at the Cleveland Museum of Art, Rorimer also spoke of the relationship of machinery to art. "The machine has come to democratize art," he said. He believed that machine art was both appropriate and necessary to America, because only quantity production could meet the needs of our technological society. Our failure was in the separation of artist and craftsman and in the general lack of artistic education in American society. Rorimer's plea for an artist-artisan was identical to that of the Arts and Crafts reformers. He said, "Today we marvel at the skill of the guild craftsmen and bemoan our fate at being thrust into an age of speed, quantity production, and inartistic baubles. Art and industry today have little in common . . . we have so far been more fascinated by [the machine's] fecundity than by the quality of its product."[15]

Rorimer saw the artist and machine operator of 1925 as separate as they had been in the late nineteenth century. "The work is executed by operators whose only incentive to feed their machines is the weekly pay envelope." His solution was not only to educate and train better designers, but also to "educate the manufacturers and proprietors of industry in the appreciation of art." In addition, by stimulating art appreciation in the public schools, Rorimer believed that American taste could be elevated. He therefore emphasized the need for public school teachers to be trained in art appreciation. If the public was uneducated in matters of taste and artistic quality, then there could be no market for the artistic creations of skilled artist-artisans. Rorimer's recognition of the need for both an educated public and well-trained designers went beyond the Arts and Crafts ideal of artistic excellence. He saw America's artistic dependence on Europe as something that could be altered, and he concluded his speech by saying, "It seems clear that if we, as a nation are to develop and mature—reach self sufficiency, we must inevitably reach the point of expressing ourselves artistically as well as materially."[16]

As an educator, artist, and manufacturer, Rorimer practiced the Arts and Crafts ideals of men like Morris and Triggs and adapted them to a modernizing American society. His own skilled craftsmen were treated with respect and were provided with the environment and appropriate materials needed to make quality products. In this way Rorimer was able to satisfy both his producers and consumers for many years.

Like the medieval organizations of craftsmen called guilds and the later nineteenth-century emulations, Rorimer-Brooks shops were divided among the various crafts, such as cabinetmaking, carving, finishing, upholstering, and drapery making. These were run by master craftsmen and also served as schools for apprentices who gave their services for an education; no money was exchanged. It was certainly no coincidence that Rorimer's company resembled its English prototypes, since he had spent a good deal of time in England and he openly praised Morris and his philosophy.[17]

England and America were by no means the only cultures affected by the crafts movements of the nineteenth and early twentieth centuries, as evidenced by the Wiener Werkstätte (Viennese Workshops). Anti-industrial art workshops where individual style and creativity were encouraged and where craftsmen had equal status to artists were the essence of both the English Arts and Crafts and the Wiener Werkstätte. The feature that separated the Werkstätte from Arts and Crafts, while relating it to the Bauhaus, was its extreme modernism. Austria was one of the birthplaces of modernism, although perhaps less well known than France or Germany. There are three aspects to the Viennese modern movement: the Secession, an artists' association that began to hold exhibitions in 1898 (which may have influenced Rorimer's 1911 artist group to borrow that name); the Kunstgewerbeschule, a teaching institution that began in 1867; and the Wiener Werkstätte, an organization of design and craft workshops emphasizing the decorative arts. Founded by designers Josef Hoffman and Kolomon Moser and backed by Fritz Waerndorfer, the Werk-

stätte spanned three decades from 1903 to 1932 and incorporated styles ranging from Art Nouveau and Art Deco to Bauhaus. But unlike the Bauhaus, the
Wiener Werkstätte refused to take the plunge into mass production. Chrono-
logically, philosophically, and stylistically the Werkstätte bridged the Arts and
Crafts, Art Nouveau, Art Deco, and Bauhaus.[18]

One explanation for the variety of styles was the emphasis placed on individual creativity in the workshops. Each artist and craftsman was encouraged
to develop his or her own style, and the objects carried the signature of both
artist-designer and craftsman. Rorimer imported, collected, and sold objects
produced by the Werkstätte and he also shared its ideals.

Even at its peak, Rorimer-Brooks never lost its Arts and Crafts flavor. The
look of its elegant Euclid Avenue showroom, which catered to an elite clientele,
hardly recalled the simplicity that Arts and Crafts stood for. Yet the philosophy
and practices retained the movement's essence. Most items were made by hand,
from drafting table to hand finishing. Craftsmen belonged to unions and op-
erated much like those in early European guilds. Apprenticeship preceded full
status, and it was not uncommon for artisans to spend their entire working
lives with the firm and to work alongside fathers, sons, and brothers. The
shops were organized to encourage workers to learn from one another and
from Rorimer, who often chose to pick up a carving tool rather than to give
verbal instructions. Occasionally an employee would be sent elsewhere to further his education, such as chief designer William B. Green, who was sent to
study at the Bauhaus at Rorimer's expense.[19]

The Bauhaus was the source of Europe's most radically modern design of
the 1920s, and by sending Green, Rorimer learned of its accomplishments.
Originally called the Weimar Kunstgewerbeschule, it was cofounded and
headed by Rorimer's friend, the Belgian designer Henri van de Velde. In 1919
the name was changed to Staatliches Bauhaus and Walter Gropius became the
new director. Architecture, painting, and sculpture were considered the central
areas of study, yet all other crafts from cabinetmaking to weaving were taught,
because one of the goals was to elevate the crafts. The predominant style was
clean and slick and devoid of ornamentation.[20]

From the beginning the school was plagued by lack of funds, internal feuds,
and hostile officials. In 1925 the Bauhaus moved to the industrial town of Dessau. One reason for the move was to attract the leaders of industry, for up
until then only an elite group of art critics appreciated the individualistic
handmade crafts. Its new goal was to combine art with industry—the same
words but with a different meaning from Arts and Crafts under Morris. Mass
production was the new form that the merger took, yet the Dessau government was still not satisfied. Adapting to industry was only part of the chal-
lenge. Because the Bauhaus had socialist leanings similar to those of the
English Arts and Crafts, it could not survive in the midst of right-wing politics.
By 1933, after succumbing to German political pressure, it closed its doors.
Although the Bauhaus graduated fewer than 500 students, it still remains a
symbol of progressive design.[21]

What Green learned during his experience at the school was the use of new materials and the techniques needed to work them in nontraditional styles. Wood was no longer the only material suited for furniture. Metals like tubular steel, aluminum, and chrome, as well as plastics and glass were appropriate for mass production of the new International Style. The Bauhaus was unique in its use of antihistorical, purely modern forms. When Green returned to Cleveland he served as the primary source for modern designs that Rorimer was starting to introduce to a reluctant audience. Pure Bauhaus designs were too radical for most Clevelanders, so Green adapted them to more familiar forms like Art Deco. Materials such as aluminum and plastics were occasionally used by Rorimer, but most Bauhaus-inspired work was for special projects unknown to the regular clientele.[22]

Another nineteenth-century movement that influenced Rorimer was the Aesthetic movement, which can be seen as an offshoot of the reformist ideology of Ruskin and Morris. It was also essentially missionary, because artists and designers worked simultaneously to improve public taste.[23] The goal was to elevate the level of design in all objects, particularly those used in interior design. The emphasis of the Aesthetic movement was on art, and terms such as *art furniture, artistic houses, art glass,* and *art pottery* became popular. Machinery was not an issue, and it was used freely providing that the results were "artistic."

An effective apostle of aestheticism and an acquaintance of Rorimer was Oscar Wilde, to whom the idea of "art for art's sake" has been credited. Up until the 1880s the content of a painting had been considered to be more important than its form, a view shared by Arts and Crafts leader Ruskin. Wilde's revolutionary concept contributed to separating the philosophy of the Aesthetic from the Arts and Crafts movement. Ruskin's preoccupation with morality and social issues in painting, and later in the applied arts, was of little interest to Wilde. But both aestheticism and the Arts and Crafts philosophy inspired designers, and together with Art Nouveau, they served as a bridge to the styles of modernism in the early twentieth century.

Art Nouveau was a visually distinctive but short-lived movement (from the 1890s until about 1910) that spread throughout most of Europe. Art Nouveau shared its typical themes, such as nymphlike females, either nude or in flowing translucent gowns, and with long swirling locks of hair, with the Symbolist painters. But Art Nouveau was primarily decorative, and its curvilinear, organic, Japanese-inspired motifs could be adapted to more rectilinear designs such as those by Charles Rennie Mackintosh of the Glasgow School, by Josef Hoffman of the Wiener Werkstätte,[24] and in Cleveland by Louis Rorimer. At the turn of the century, Rorimer's head wood-carver, James Fillous, carved interior architectural features in the Art Nouveau style. Such sumptuous carving was desirable, yet rare, in Cleveland.[25]

Rorimer personally knew prominent Art Nouveau artistic personalities such as illustrator Aubrey Beardsley and glass designers Louis Comfort Tiffany, René Lalique, and Émile Gallé. Their work was promoted in the Paris shop of Siegfried Bing, another of Rorimer's acquaintances. Beginning in 1895 Bing's shop, L'Art Nouveau, which gave the style its name, was a showcase for some of the most innovative examples.[26] The poet Gertrude Stein was among the many other friends and acquaintances Rorimer visited while in Europe. Unfortunately, he regarded her collection of Picasso paintings as part of a fad that had already run its course.[27] What Rorimer absorbed during five years of European study was a mixture of traditional art history and the most avant-garde trends being practiced by individuals in and out of the schools. Rorimer developed much of his early artistic philosophy while sitting at café tables discussing the influence of William Morris, of Auguste Rodin, Paul Cézanne, and Camille Pissaro.[28]

After returning to Cleveland Rorimer kept ties with Europe, the major source of style in American decorative arts. He sailed to France, Germany, and England, sometimes as often as twice a year, and visited Italy, Spain, Switzerland, and Scandinavia. His travels also included Morocco, Egypt, Mexico, and South America. When in Europe he would meet old friends, artists, teachers, and business associates and return to Cleveland each time with both fresh ideas and antiques from old castles.[29]

Because few Americans with an eye for artistic innovation and quality visited Europe as regularly as Rorimer did, he was among the first to introduce the work of several contemporary European designers to America. For example, Rorimer is believed to have brought the first Rembrandt Bugatti bronzes to America. He has also been credited with being the first to introduce Lalique glass to America, in 1904, long before it was produced on a large scale.[30] This is possible, because René Lalique began experimenting with pieces made completely of glass, such as vases and panels, around 1900. Prior to that time, his use of glass was for multimedia pieces and jewelry. By 1902 he had a small glassworks that employed four workers. His first commercial glass commission began in 1907 for the perfumer François Coty, and it was not until 1912 that Coty offered Lalique bottles in New York.[31] Rorimer's early association with Siegfried Bing in Paris gave him adequate opportunity to become acquainted with Lalique's work prior to 1904, because Bing had been instrumental in promoting Art Nouveau glass in his shop.

Many of Rorimer's friends and acquaintances were associated with his business and his role as an interior designer. Others were found through his role of teacher, which spanned twenty years. When he returned home to Cleveland in 1895, the Cleveland School of Art was located in the old Kelley Mansion, a large brick mid-Victorian building at 1001 Wilson Avenue (now East Fifty-fifth Street near Prospect Avenue). Herman Matzen, who had studied sculpture in Germany and joined the school in 1887, saw an architectural modeling and design instructor in Rorimer. From 1898 to 1918 Rorimer taught at the Cleveland School of Art, and together with Henry G. Keller, he organized the educational plan used for many years at the school.[32]

Until 1904 Rorimer taught modeling and casting in the Kelley stables, which had been remodeled for his classroom. In 1905 the school was given a permanent home at 11441 Juniper Road. By then he had established himself as an interior designer, so it suited both the school (where it is said that he would not accept any salary)[33] and his own business that Rorimer teach decorative design and eventually supervise the design and interior decorative department. Throughout his stay at the Cleveland School of Art, Rorimer combined the teaching of theory with practice. Among his students were the renowned watercolorist Charles Burchfield, illustrator Carl Broemel, sculptor Max Kalish, painters Ferdinand Burgdorff and Abel Warshawsky, Horrace E. Potter, Jane Carson Barron, and *Plain Dealer* critic Grace Kelly.[34]

When a very youthful-looking twenty-six-year-old Rorimer began teaching at the Cleveland School of Art, he was little older than his students, who found it necessary to test his authority. As he entered his architectural modeling class for the first time, a ball of clay came flying through the air and landed flat on his left cheek. The class sat silently, waiting for Rorimer's reaction. After scraping the glob of clay from his cheek, he forced a smile and calmly replied, "Gentlemen, this is not a class in practical politics, so we'll refrain from throwing any more mud. Besides, it's a poor way of molding anything, even opinion."[35] It was the last clay ball thrown in his class. Although he never forgot the incident, Rorimer made no attempt to learn by whom the clay ball had been thrown. Many years later, his friend Abel Warshawsky, who became Cleveland's leading Impressionist painter, approached Rorimer saying that he was compelled to tell him that he had thrown the ball of clay. The little confession satisfied Warshawsky's conscience more than Rorimer's curiosity.

Recalling the 1898 modeling class, Warshawsky wrote in his autobiography:

> Our modeling instructor, a handsome young man with a profile like Julius Caesar, had studied for years in Munich and Paris. He seemed to us endowed with a marvellous facility for transforming with a few magic touches a lump of clay into something alive and beautiful. How mature and sedate he seemed to me, though now I realize he was only a little older than his pupils. We loved him for his friendliness and lack of condescension, for in his dealings with us there was no hampering feeling of master and pupil. He seemed to be one of us, only richer in experience and general proficiency. Though he never marked his superiority, we inevitably came to feel it.[36]

Teaching and sponsoring young artists was one way in which Rorimer could contribute to the beauty in his world. A contemporary journalist noted that "The number of outstanding designers, artists, sculptors, and painters whom he has developed and aided, both in the classroom and outside, constitutes a list of considerable length." According to Viktor Schreckengost, noted Cleveland artist and Rorimer's friend, Rorimer was "such a grand man, so nice, so sweet, so interested in young people and getting them started."[37] Rorimer sometimes offered young artists a chance to free-lance their designs with his company. For example, after Schreckengost graduated from the Cleveland School of Art, he went to study in Austria. When he returned to Cleveland, Rorimer hired him to design a new ashtray for the Statler Hotels. Schrecken-

14

gost's ashtrays were black outside with brightly colored interiors, but when they were manufactured in Sebring, Ohio, there was no slot to hold the cigarettes. The thousands of ashtrays would have caused embarrassment, if not considerable damage from cigarettes falling out, but they were very attractive, so Rorimer used them in the hotel lobbies to hold popcorn and peanuts.[38]

Rorimer often remarked how much he had enjoyed teaching at the Cleveland School of Art. Perhaps that is why his role as teacher carried over to the shops of Rorimer-Brooks, where he literally kept his hand in everything. A designer working on a rendering might be interrupted by Rorimer, who thought nothing of adding his own touches to the drawing. His craftsmen must have had many exercises in patience by the time they learned Rorimer's favorite saying, "When in doubt, make it simple." (For hotels, his motto was, "When in doubt, paint it red.") Head woodcarver John Nepodal was once working on a piece with acanthus leaves, on which he had painstakingly executed delicate tendrils weaving in and out. Rorimer calmly picked up a knife and sliced off the tendrils. "Too fussy, John," he explained and walked away.[39]

A number of Rorimer's better students at the Cleveland School of Art joined his design studio and worked for him. For example, in addition to the design and manufacture of home furnishings, Rorimer employed skilled silversmiths who made jewelry and other metal items and sold them under the name Rokesley Shop from about 1907 to 1916. The Rokesley name was derived from combining letters from the names [Ro]rheimer, Bla[kes]lee, and Smed[ley]. Mary Blakeslee and Ruth Smedley were among the artists and exhibitors. A beautiful silver tea and coffee service with ebony handles, semiprecious stones, and embossed and chased ornament was designed by Rorimer and executed by Rokesley. The set was featured in a major Arts and Crafts exhibit in 1987.[40] In 1909, when Rorimer Studios was located at 1907–31 East Ninth Street, the Rokesley Shop was at 1931 East Ninth Street. In the 1909 *Exhibition Catalogue* of the Cleveland Architectural Club, items 642 to 669 by the Rokesley Shop were made mostly of silver, but also included materials such as gold, enamel copper, and semiprecious stones. Six of these items, made of silver, copper, and brass, were pictured in the catalog.[41]

Rorimer's first priority in any art form was beauty and harmony, so the effect of copper or brass, such as that used by the Rokesley Shop, could be as pleasing as that of silver or gold. While addressing the National Council of Jewish Women at their Autumn Social in 1903, he said, "The intrinsic value of an article has nothing to do with its value as an ornament."[42]

As Rorimer recognized the usefulness and potential beauty in different materials, he also saw the value in selecting from a wide range of both historic and modern styles. Since his Paris school days Rorimer had become a modernist, while continuing to acknowledge the artistic riches of history. From this viewpoint, modernism was not a passing fad, but an attitude, an ability to see art as a dynamic force changing and progressing with time, while remaining a clear expression of its period. To Rorimer, a modernist never ceases to be a modernist, and he can recognize modernity even as it occurred in centuries

15

past. Historic styles were once modern, and Rorimer would not ignore an artistic element simply because it was old. Neither would he expect the windows of a contemporary building to be small because there had been a tax on window openings five hundred years ago or because glass was rare and costly when it was first used.[43] He believed that as long as the past is not misused, it can serve us by adapting to current needs.

Adapting to current needs was the key to Rorimer's early success. Rather than dictate his personal taste, Rorimer was sensitive to the conditions of a growing city. His recognition of the common desire for traditional interiors, his connoisseurship of historic style, and his insistence upon quality were the elements needed to establish Rorimer-Brooks as a major interior design firm. Once he became established, Rorimer incorporated new designs and offered them to a fashion-conscious clientele. Items displayed in his showrooms were often the products of his travels and the pursuance of his education. An important means by which Rorimer continued to educate himself and others was through his organizational activities. Associations with other artists and businessmen provided an exchange of ideas that enabled Rorimer to continue to adapt to current needs.

⚜ 2 ⚜

CULTURE

Rorimer had direct access to the front line of design innovation through his contacts in cultural organizations. He not only contributed to Cleveland's artistic development through his leadership in Cleveland-based organizations, he also brought back word of national and international advancements when he traveled. Rorimer's cultural participation served as a network whereby he could teach one group what he had learned from another. By opening channels between various associations, Rorimer helped to connect the local, national, and international levels of the art world.

His interests went beyond the visual arts, because Rorimer was also involved in music, literature, and theater. He had the admirable ability to combine business with pleasure, and his extensive cultural involvement benefited both his company and his lively social life—he and his wife Edith entertained guests at their "house in the woods" by throwing lavish dinner parties. Rorimer was not a man who kept to himself, as the following list of organizational memberships will attest.

The two major art institutions in his hometown were the Cleveland Museum of Art and the Cleveland School of Art, and Rorimer was active in both. The Cleveland Art Association, the Cleveland Society of Artists, and the Cleveland Architectural Club were other art organizations to which he belonged. Rorimer's local interests outside of the visual arts included the Cleveland Playhouse, the Cleveland Orchestra, the Rowfant Club, the Cleveland Chamber of Commerce and Mid-Day Club, Oakwood Country Club, and the Western Reserve Historical Society. In New York City his memberships included the American Union of Decorative Artists and Craftsmen (AUDAC), the Metropolitan Museum of Art, the Salamagundi Club, and the Art-In-Trades Club. He also belonged to the Arts Club of Washington, D.C. Nationally, Rorimer was a member of the American Institute of Architects, the American Institute of Decorators, the American Federation of Arts, the Archaeological Institute of America, the Association of Arts and Industries, and he served as a director

17

of the Statler Hotel Corporation. On the international level, he was one of 108 Americans appointed by the secretary of commerce, Herbert Hoover, to travel to L'Exposition des Arts Décoratifs et Industriels Modernes in Paris in 1925.

Rorimer's first opportunity to participate and exhibit in an art organization was with his first partner, M. James Bowman. The Cleveland Architectural Club had been organized in 1894 with fourteen charter members. In 1896 there were forty-seven members, including Rorimer and Bowman, who took part in the first annual exhibition.

The exhibition catalog featured a full-page photograph of "A Gothic Den" and "Louis XVI Boudoir" by Rohrheimer and Bowman Studios, plus a "Foreign Sketch" by Rorimer. By the second annual exhibition, in 1897, Rorimer was an officer of the current work committee and was one of seven on the exhibition committee. Bowman had moved to Chicago and exhibited with Rorimer as a nonmember of the Architectural Club. The "German Renaissance Interior" illustrated in the catalog was a Rohrheimer and Bowman design, while others, such as the "Flemish Renaissance Reception Hall," plaster casts of "Faun Head" and "Heraldic Design," and a dozen other entries (not illustrated in the catalog) were by Rorimer alone.[1] All of Rorimer's design themes were popular with American architects and designers at the close of the century, and all were inspired by European historic architectural styles from Medieval to early nineteenth-century Neoclassicism. Because reformers had discredited later nineteenth-century Romantic revivals, Victorian styles were avoided. Many of the Gothic and Renaissance motifs Rorimer selected were derived from those he had studied at the Kunstgewerbeschule or had casually recorded in his sketchbook while walking along the streets of Munich in the early 1890s.

Rohrheimer and Hays participated in the third annual exhibition of the Cleveland Architectural Club, in 1900. Their contributions were still Gothic and Renaissance designs, because these were still considered to be appropriate by the profession. The Architectural League of America, of which the Cleveland Architectural Club was a part, sought to promote American architecture and the allied fine and applied arts. Although their selections for the exhibition appear to have all been in European historic styles, the purposes of the league were "to encourage an indigenous and inventive architecture and to lead architectural thought to modern sources of inspiration."[2] What was wishful thinking in 1900 would soon become realized, and Rorimer would actively participate in the movement toward modernism.

By the fourth annual exhibition, in 1901, Rorimer was vice-president of the Cleveland Architectural Club and vice-chairman of its exhibition and finance committees. His exhibits were with his new partner, Louis Hays, and all of the designs were for a Cincinnati residence.[3]

European historic styles inspired most of Rorimer's early designs, and his European travels enhanced his usefulness to cultural institutions at home. The art and antiques markets were major attractions for Rorimer when he traveled, and he always returned home to Cleveland with new acquisitions. Rorimer-

18

Brooks and his considerable private collection were the greatest beneficiaries of these buying trips, but, for example, he also brought portraits of literary men and artists to hang at the Rowfant Club, and he made purchases for the Cleveland Museum of Art.

In a 1925 letter to Rorimer, Theodore Sizer, the curator of prints and Oriental art at the Cleveland Museum of Art, suggested that Rorimer purchase some eighteenth-century prints and other material from the Louvre in Paris. Sizer added that "Mr. Ivins, of the Metropolitan Museum, said that he thought their things are so important that he is going to arrange for a fund in order to buy a great block of them so as to illustrate the development of ornament, architecture, costume, formal gardens, and that sort of thing. If you have the Museum at all in mind, anything that you picked out would, of course, be acceptable."[4]

From this excerpt it is evident that Rorimer's artistic judgment was highly regarded. Sizer also recommended a particular Parisian print dealer for purchasing prints by artists such as Honoré Daumier. He told Rorimer that this dealer "is a very nice fellow, and I know you would like him. Most of the other print dealers in Paris are the Fifth Avenue variety, and are to be avoided by the man who knows his business."[5] Evidently, Rorimer knew his business, judging by the art and antiques he bought and sold during his lifetime and the impressive collection dispersed by his estate after his death (see chapter 3).

Rorimer assisted with museum acquisitions on numerous occasions, and he corresponded with curators and museum directors such as Frederic Allen Whiting, of the Cleveland Museum of Art, until 1930, and William M. Millikin, who followed Whiting as a director. For example, Whiting was once interested in a group of photographs and drawings of furniture. In 1920 he wrote to Rorimer, "It occurs to me that the drawings might be unusually valuable and that you might be interested while in New York to go over them with [the owner] and report as to their usefulness to the Museum and the school. It also occurs to me that if these are an important acquisition, you might be able to induce some people to subscribe to a fund for their purchase for the Museum."[6] Not only was Rorimer's opinion solicited by the museum, it is likely that he played a role in raising funds. His contacts through organizational affiliations and his well-heeled clientele undoubtedly were supporters of the museum.

Rorimer worked with Theodore Sizer to acquire part of a print collection belonging to Professor Paul Joseph Sachs. In 1925 Sachs had given or bequeathed his entire collection of prints and drawings to Harvard University. Sizer arranged with him to purchase the duplicates for the Cleveland Museum of Art at the prices Sachs had originally paid for them twenty years earlier. There were other prints that Sizer was "in desperate need of," and Rorimer was asked to assist with their acquisition as well.[7]

His friendship with directors and staff members of the Cleveland Museum of Art and his seat on the Advisory Council were only part of Rorimer's enduring relationship with the museum, since Rorimer-Brooks filled part of the museum's decorating needs and lent and exhibited furniture. In 1915 Rorimer installed the wall coverings and fixtures for the various museum galleries. He used a natural color in monk's cloth "guaranteeing the best of materials and first class workmanship throughout." Window shades of holland cloth, traverse tracks, and linen curtains were also installed throughout the building. Other examples of interior work done for the museum were velvet curtains in 1918, some of which were gifts of Rorimer-Brooks.[8]

The Cleveland Museum also worked with Rorimer-Brooks through its employees, such as chief designer William B. Green. The casual tone of letters between Green and museum staff members suggests a friendly and personal relationship. For example, in a 1923 letter discussing upholstery fabric for several sets of chairs, a staff member told Green to "come out again and see us when you get fagged with too much R.B."[9] Other informal correspondence was exchanged frequently between Rorimer-Brooks and the museum. Director William Millikin wrote to Rorimer in Palm Beach, Florida, where he was recuperating from ill health in 1936.[10] On another occasion, Henry Sayles Francis, the curator of paintings, also wrote to Rorimer's Florida address to congratulate him on the marriage of his daughter Louise to violinist Samuel Dushkin, to wish him a speedy recovery, and to thank him for the Warshawsky portrait he had given to the museum.[11]

A more publicly known association with the art museum was the series of Rorimer-Brooks exhibits in the Cleveland May Show. This annual exhibition of work done by Cleveland-area artists and craftsmen was designed specifically to encourage local talent as well as collectors. From the beginning, the Cleveland May Show was a significant regional show in terms of both its size and quality. When the first annual May Show was held in 1919, it was supervised by Millikin, then curator of decorative arts and later museum director from 1930 to 1958. At that time, businesses as well as individuals could enter, and Rorimer-Brooks exhibited six pieces of furniture.

Three of these pieces—the "Italian Seat," designed jointly by Rorimer and Green, the "English Console" designed by Green and C. M. Hawk, and the "Round Italian Table" designed by Green and Antoniac Amendale—were executed by the same craftsmen. Fred Wittmus, head of the cabinet shop in the 1920s, was the cabinetmaker; Rudolph Voelker did the carving; Ulrich Leber, head of the finishing shop, did the finishing work; and James Gavin, head of the upholstery shop, was the upholsterer. First prize for furniture was awarded to a fourth piece, "English Sideboard," which was pictured in the *Bulletin of the Cleveland Museum of Art* in 1919. Green designed this two-doored, three-drawered, historically inspired piece that displayed both seventeenth- and eighteenth-century elements. The turned front legs and generally boxy form recall late seventeenth-century design, although the proportions are of a later date. Sideboards did not come into fashion until the late eighteenth century, so this sideboard was not intended to appear like a period piece. Its combination of stylistic features from different periods was not due to ignorance, since Rorimer's designers were versed in history. Their intention was to create original and aesthetically pleasing designs while working within a traditional framework. The final Rorimer-Brooks entry in the show, the "Long Italian Console," was given a commendation and was designed by Rorimer and Green.[12]

In the next May Show, in 1920, Rorimer-Brooks again took first prize for furniture. Green and Rorimer designed the "Italian Couch," a fully upholstered three-cushioned couch with a repeating pattern of pierced carving across the front. This was illustrated in the 1920 *Bulletin*. Two other pieces exhibited in that show were a "William and Mary Walnut Table" and the "Italian Round Table," which was designed by Rorimer and Amendale.[13]

Two years later, in 1922, Rorimer-Brooks again took first prize for furniture in the show. The "English Sideboard" designed by Green and executed by Wittmus and Leber was nearly identical to the sideboard of 1919. The only significant additions were four mythological figures carved with crossed arms, which are very similar to some drawings in Rorimer's Munich student sketchbook. As with the first sideboard, Green, and not Rorimer, designed the piece, but Rorimer certainly influenced his use of the carved figures, since he closely oversaw all work done at his studio. In the next year's show, in 1923, Green's design of the "Walnut and Burl Table Desk" again took first prize for furniture. Rorimer's design "Decorated Walnut Chest" took second prize the following year. Green and Rorimer jointly took a prize for their design of the "Long Carved Chest" in 1925. The last years in which the museum's *Bulletin* notes a Rorimer-Brooks entry were 1926 and 1928.[14]

These entries, from 1919 to 1928, gave Rorimer exposure and prestige and influenced the viewing public with his selection of furniture styles. Tastes of the judges who accepted entries and awarded prizes and of the artists, designers, and craftsmen who entered the May Show had an impact on the local art scene. Rorimer-Brooks dominated the furniture portion of the show during an important decade in Cleveland's history. Industrial money supported a wave of both urban and suburban expansion in Cleveland in the 1920s. Many of these participants in the city's growth visited the annual May Show, saw Rorimer endorsed by the experts, and then sought him out to furnish their homes and offices. The number of residential interiors executed by Rorimer-Brooks was a small fraction of the total during this period, but the number that felt his influence was great. In 1929 a journalist wrote that "the hands of Louis Rorimer, modernist, may be seen in thousands of interiors, although his organization may not have done so much as hung a curtain." In fact, Rorimer's influence was not only local, since he had become "a national figure in the field of interior decoration."[15]

When Rorimer died, the museum praised him for both his artistic achievements and his generosity: "From the earliest inception of the Museum, he was deeply interested in its welfare. In all those years he had never failed to contribute annually to its support, establishing on December 6, 1937, The Louis Rorimer Membership Endowment Fund, and it was characteristic of the man that during his lifetime he had made provision that, upon his death, a substantial addition should be made to that fund."[16] Certainly the artistic achievements that the museum spoke of included Rorimer's prominence in the May

Show and the Cleveland School of Art. The Cleveland May Show was the highlight of the contemporary art scene in the area and also served as a bridge between local artists and the Cleveland Museum of Art. The show was dominated by the Cleveland School of Art (now the Cleveland Institute of Art) and in turn gave the school a highly respected arena in which to display the work of its faculty and students outside of the school's own exhibition gallery.

Rorimer also had another vehicle by which he could influence taste. His own exhibits naturally influenced the art-conscious public, and his contact with numerous Cleveland School of Art students indirectly promoted the artistic beliefs he held at the moment. In the early years of the twentieth century, teacher-student relationships were not particularly flexible. Instructors' styles were often recognizable in their students' work, and only later, when and if students in turn became artists and teachers, did their individuality become pronounced. Even an artist's mature personal style displayed elements acquired as a student.

Rorimer loved to teach, and he shared his talents with art students for twenty years. Although he retired in 1919 from teaching architectural modeling, design, and interior decoration, he kept in close contact with the school by serving continuously as an advisory board member on the instruction committee until 1932 and as a trustee until his death in 1939. Rorimer said that his days teaching at the Cleveland School of Art were among the happiest in his life.[17]

Because most of his own formal education had taken place in Munich and Paris, what he passed along to his students in Cleveland had a European flavor. A sample of Rorimer's own student work has survived. Two sketchbooks from the Kunstgewerbeschule in Munich are filled with pencil sketches of architectural motifs from Gothic and Renaissance buildings and furniture and a few Rococo designs, some of which are accented in watercolor. A collection of small watercolor paintings was found with the belongings of his son, James. These are unsigned, as are most student exercises, but are almost certainly examples of Rorimer's early student work. Several formal class projects done at the Kunstgewerbeschule and dated 1891 and 1894 are evidence of his skill with pen and ink. These meticulous drawings demonstrate both his drawing skill and his early interest in architecture and interior and exterior architectural detail. Included are exercises executed in pen and ink with the addition of light ink washes demonstrating his early experimentation with simple geometric shapes and patterns. Although no later work other than furniture design and carving has yet been uncovered, this does not necessarily indicate that Rorimer did not continue to draw and paint. His close associations with other artists, especially painters, such as members of the Secessionists, the Cleveland Society of Artists, and the Cleveland Art Association, suggest that Rorimer continued to paint as well.

The Cleveland Art Association was organized in 1915 and incorporated in 1916 in order to promote art and artists in Cleveland. Members held exhibitions and lectures, sponsored the Arts and Crafts Guild for graduate students

Ink drawing from Rorimer's student portfolio, Munich, 1891. *Courtesy of the Rorimer family.*

23

Ink drawing from Rorimer's student portfolio, Munich, 1891. *Courtesy of the Rorimer family.*

of the Cleveland School of Art, awarded scholarships to the school, and offered a European fellowship. They purchased work by Cleveland artists for the permanent collection of the Cleveland Museum of Art, contributed to its library, and cooperated with its education department. This first annual Cleveland May Show was originally proposed by the Cleveland Art Association in order to provide local artists with increased support. Rorimer's membership included holding the office of vice-president in 1932 and 1933.[18]

Another Cleveland art organization was the long-lived Cleveland Society of Artists, which disbanded in 1983. It was conceived on January 8, 1913, when

24

six artists met "in the furtherance of a place to organize Cleveland Artists into a body for the betterment of Art Conditions in Cleveland." The following week, they met to prepare a list of artists who might share their purpose, one of whom was Rorimer. On May 28, 1913, their monthly meeting was held at the Hotel Statler, where Rorimer was one of the guest speakers at a banquet dinner. Among the members at that time were both current and future friends and associates of Rorimer such as Ihna Thayer Frary, R. Guy Cowan, Herman Matzen, August Biehle, W. B. Green, and James Fillous. Rorimer joined the club no later than November 14, 1914, when he was first listed as an attending member. Between February 26, 1915, and March 19, 1915, the club's name was changed from the Cleveland Arts Club to the Society of Cleveland Artists. Then at the May 26, 1916, meeting, a proposal was made to change the name to the Cleveland Society of Artists. On November 17, 1916, Rorimer was appointed by the chair as advisory member of the entertainment committee, and at the December 1, 1916, regular meeting he gave a talk on "Decorative Art."[19]

The society grew with the help of charter members like Rorimer, and in 1921 it became incorporated. Rorimer held the office of president in 1920 and 1921. Exhibitions and sales of art and eventually a permanent collection were housed in their East Eighty-eighth Street location. Rorimer instituted the practice of holding art auctions with the proceeds going toward granting scholarships to students at the Cleveland School of Art. The society's belief in the promotion of Cleveland artists went so far as to form a "Cleveland First" committee. They saw a lack of local pride and wrote, "As matters stand at present and have always stood in Cleveland's history, a Clevelander's work is handicapped in Cleveland, merely because it is done by a Clevelander!"[20] The committee sought recognition of superior work in all lines of endeavor, urged consideration of Clevelanders by Clevelanders, and encouraged the formation of similar committees within other local organizations.

Rorimer remained active in the Cleveland Society of Artists until his death in 1939, when its monthly publication, *Silhouette*, published a photo of Rorimer and an obituary. He is described as "a warm friend and advisor of our Society and a most generous donor, both of time and money, to the organization. His two years of presidency and his many years as a council member were of great value to the healthy growth of our club."[21] In a eulogy delivered by Rorimer's lifelong friend and colleague, Ihna Thayer Frary, he said: "Those of us who have been associated with him, as members of the Cleveland Society of Artists, remember with gratitude how his business acumen was a means of working out the plans by which its club house was financed and made possible. As president of this society . . . and as an officer in many other organizations related to various arts, his judgment and executive ability were called upon endlessly for assistance when problems financial or artistic were to be solved."[22]

Rorimer was also interested in books and literature, music, and the performing arts. One organization to which he belonged was the Rowfant Club, founded on February 29, 1892, by a group of Cleveland book lovers and collectors. Evidence of Rorimer's love of books can be seen in letters written from

Munich to his brother-in-law Abe in 1891. Besides lists of books included in his expense accounts, Rorimer requested money to buy more books. Later, an extensive art library was shelved at Rorimer-Brooks. This was minor compared to his personal collection, much of which was later presented to the Metropolitan Museum of Art.[23]

The purpose of the Rowfant Club was to study the technical aspects of bookmaking and collecting, as well as literature, and the club also published fine-quality limited editions. Its membership was confined to men with literary and collecting interests, with a limit of 150 residents and 55 nonresidents by invitation only. Beginning in 1895 the club was housed at 3028 Prospect Avenue (formerly 766 Prospect Street). It issued an annual *Yearbook,* was governed by elected officers, and a fifteen-man Council of Fellows was elected for staggered three-year terms. In 1933 and again in 1936 Rorimer was elected to the council. He served on the house committee in 1937–38 and was elected president for the 1932–33 term.[24]

Presidency of a much different kind of cultural institution, the Cleveland Playhouse, was also Rorimer's from 1932 to 1934, and his picture hangs today in the hall of former presidents. By the late 1920s the Cleveland Playhouse was "one of the most successful as well as one of the most distinguished Little Theatres in the country."[25] Having outgrown its makeshift quarters, a new building was designed in 1926 by the well-known Cleveland architects Philip Lindsley Small and Charles Bacon Rowley. The theater of the new Playhouse building was to be unique with its two auditoriums and two stages with seating capacities of 500 and 200. Among the rooms of the Playhouse building planned for other activities was the Green Room, which was designed, furnished, and donated by Rorimer-Brooks. Completed in 1927, the Green Room reflected Rorimer's recent exposure to Art Moderne design in Paris. Tables, benches, sofas, and chairs were extremely modern, yet with a hint of neoclassicism in their repeated use of vertical reeding and fluting. Unusual tub-shaped chairs with straight fluted back splats extending to the floor resembled Parisian examples from the 1920s. Unfortunately, all that has survived of the original interior is one two-doored rectilinear Art Deco cabinet in the same red mahogany finish as the room's wood paneling, which was featured in a 1927 article about the Playhouse in *Architectural Record.*[26]

Rorimer, who had long been associated with the Playhouse, was elected to the office of vice-president for two consecutive terms before becoming president in 1932, also for two terms. A contemporary journalist described Rorimer's role as president: "He is glad to be known as an active, not acting, president of the Play House. In fact, he takes an interest in the Play House management so active that some days find him dividing his time between his business and the theater."[27] Rorimer voiced opinions about the theater and about his office as Playhouse president. Among the issues that he strongly believed in and supported were the production of manuscript plays and the encouragement of unknown authors. Rorimer felt that "the most enduring manifestations of art spring from the soil" and that theater productions "should make a greater appeal to the masses than to the classes."[28] This populist attitude may be surprising when expressed by a man whose business catered to an elite clientele. But there was no inconsistency in his values, because Rorimer was making a statement specifically about the performing arts.

The quality of a play, he believed, need not be compromised by appealing to a broad audience. On the contrary, its ability to reach many would be to its credit. Neither the writer nor the performer necessarily puts forth more effort to deliver a performance to a popular audience than to a special group of insiders. Decorative arts, on the other hand, must be delivered on a one-to-one basis, with the exception of those pieces exhibited in a museum. A dining room set, for example, can serve only one household at a time. If it is to be of high quality, it must combine costly materials and workmanship. This quality would indeed become compromised if the set were intended to reach a mass audience, because it would then need to be mass-produced. With few exceptions, Rorimer could not justify the practice of mass production in his own company, and he earned the reputation for having the highest standards for his furniture. Rorimer was a lover of art in its various forms, and his highest priorities were beauty and quality, yet he recognized the limitations inherent in each art form. While he believed it desirable for a theatrical performance to reach a large audience, interior furnishings could serve only a limited group if they were to maintain high standards of workmanship.

High standards in interior decoration were the focus of the Art-In-Trades Club, a New-York based organization to which Rorimer belonged. In order to achieve these standards in decorating and furnishing, the club emphasized the need for education, and it sponsored lectures, exhibits, and demonstrations. When the club was organized in 1906 its objectives were stated as follows: "To bring into association men engaged in or interested in the Arts and Art Trades for mutual advancement and study; to study the principles of art as applied to trades connected with the decoration and furnishing of buildings; to harmonize commercial activity with the growing art tendencies of the present time; to foster feeling for taste . . . and to strengthen the natural bond between those thus allied."[29] Bringing professionals together for the study and advancement of interior decoration was a pioneering idea at this early date. The idea was well received, and by 1923 the Art-in-Trades Club established a permanent clubhouse with facilities for lectures, meetings, dining, and even sleeping. Rorimer was photographed with members of the club at the annual dinner held at the Hotel Astor in New York on April 11, 1918.[30] His membership is evidence of Rorimer's early leadership and commitment to the profession at the national level.

Charter membership in organizations to which Rorimer belonged is indicative of his role as a leader. One such organization was the short-lived (1928–32) American Union of Decorative Artists and Craftsmen (AUDAC), with headquarters in New York City. According to the *Architectural Record*, "the purpose of this society is to give direction to contemporary design in America, particularly as it applies to industry." As stated in the preamble of its constitution, "the undoubted benefits which the world has derived from the development of machine industry and the spread of popular education, have been accompanied by certain unfortunate effects. It is evident to most of us that the more obvious of these effects are the discrepancy between the life of the people today and the setting in which it is lived, and the inappropriateness of one to the other."[31] Rorimer's philosophy regarding comfort and practicality of interiors was consistent with this statement.

The goal of AUDAC was to help remedy this discrepancy between modern lifestyles and traditional, historically-based interior environments, because twentieth-century life should have its own characteristic setting. AUDAC's method of promoting modern design was the exhibition, such as the major one held at the Brooklyn Museum from June through September in 1931, in which 70 of its 117 active members displayed decorative and industrial art. Exhibits included furniture by top names in radical modern design such as Donald Desky, Paul Frankl, Norman Bel Geddes, Hugo Gnam, Eugene Schoen, Joseph Urban, Kem Weber, and Frank Lloyd Wright. There were accessories by Russel Wright and fabrics by Ruth Reeves, to mention only two. The work was all designed especially for the exhibit in order to illustrate the newest in American design philosophy. Although Rorimer was an active member of the organization and considered to be a pioneer of modern art in America, it is not known why he did not participate in the exhibit.[32]

American modernity was the dominant theme, because the goal was a single national style suited to contemporary American life rather than a European copy. (Ironically, there were so many German-born members that meetings were often held in German.) Until this time, American designers had almost always followed European leads for anything more than provincial or folk design. The time was ripe, according to AUDAC designers, to elevate American design standards by developing "a distinctive, practical and beautiful style rather than many conflicting vogues."[33] This singular style proposed by AUDAC would become America's contribution to international modern design. The combination of function and aesthetics would change the face of American interiors over the next thirty years.

The *Annual of American Design 1931*, produced and published by AUDAC, also furthered the cause by illustrating members' work and including essays explaining their philosophy. In one of the essays, the noted critic Lewis Mumford observed, "Whatever the policies of a country may be, the machine is a communist! . . . The machine . . . if properly used, will do away with industrial slavery and create, for every member of the community, an equal share in the essentials of life."[34] Mumford saw that through standardization in the industrial arts, there are two possible outcomes. The least desirable result had already been seen in the nineteenth century—this was the era of machine-made art and superficial ornamentation, which prompted the complaints of the Arts and Crafts reformers. Mumford believed that the new machine-made art must focus on utility, simplicity, and form. Innovative manufacturing techniques combined with aesthetically pleasing designs appropriate to the changing lifestyles of the American people made up the formula offered by Mumford and AUDAC.

Rorimer had seen the need for utility, simplicity, and form six years earlier when he remarked, "The key note of the future development of this applied art will be Simplicity. Owing to the high cost of labor our designers must make color and form count, rather than intricate ornament."[35] The only difference in the meaning of the term *simplify* used by Rorimer and by AUDAC was one of degree.

Paul Frankl's thoughts, also expressed in the *Annual of American Design 1931*, contained more than speculation, because he had already risen to the ranks of one of America's leading industrial designers and was in a position to practice what he preached. Many of his observations were no different from those made by Rorimer at an earlier date. Echoing Rorimer, Frankl wrote, "True modernism . . . aims to satisfy the needs of modern living and to express the spirit and the flexibility of modern life."[36] Rorimer had been quoted on more than one occasion on the need for practicality and comfort in our home environments.[37] He was a man who liked to sit back and smoke his pipe or to read in bed, and he assumed that others liked to do the same. But Frankl's description of the modern home as "a more or less harmonious assemblage of machine-made parts" and his prediction that "we shall be able to discard our old home as we discard an old set of clothes"[38] were among the most radical and economically impractical statements made by an AUDAC spokesman. Frankl was an extremist and Rorimer was a moderate, yet the basis of their aesthetic philosophy and even of some of their designs was similar. Rorimer's major disagreement with Frankl and his school was over the call to discard the old to make way for the new. With hindsight it was clear, Rorimer insisted, that some of the biggest blunders in interior design and decoration were caused by a lack of understanding and appreciation of the past. Rorimer had once remarked, "As the man who seeks to express himself as a writer must study the classics so must the artist learn the secrets of inspiration of other days. From the assimilation of earlier ideas of others comes his own power of production."[39] Rorimer had too much love and respect for history and its designs and lessons to be so presumptuous as to suppose that his latest whims were unconditionally better than anything from the past.

A second intention of AUDAC was to combat design piracy, which was presenting a problem for the industrial arts. Manufacturers had become accustomed to borrowing traditional designs, but when they began to borrow original modern designs, this practice threatened the livelihood of the designs' creators. In their efforts to solve this problem, AUDAC was instrumental in organizing the League for Suppression of Design Piracy, which advocated the passage of the Vestal Design Copyright Bill by the U.S. House of Representatives.[40]

Rorimer had expressed sentiments similar to those of AUDAC regarding both anti-design piracy and pro-American modernism. However, neither the Brooklyn Museum exhibit nor the *Design Annual* mention him as being an exhibitor. This is a curious omission considering Rorimer's philosophy and abilities as a designer. He was a charter member of AUDAC and was designing furniture in an unquestionably modern style at the same time that the other members were exhibiting their work. In fact, Rorimer had business dealings with members such as Frankl, Urban, and Bel Geddes. Rorimer had purchased fabric from Frankl; Rorimer's interior design of the St. Regis Hotel included a Joseph Urban room; and Bel Geddes was hired as a consultant when Rorimer did the Art Deco-style Manhattan Room in the Pennsylvania Hotel, also in New York.[41] When Rorimer designed his own modern furniture for the home of Homer H. Johnson (father of architect Philip Johnson) in Pinehurst, North Carolina, he also used modern pieces by members of AUDAC. Whether Rorimer was not invited to exhibit at the Brooklyn Museum or whether he declined remains unknown.

Just about the time that AUDAC dissolved, a new organization was formed—the American Institute of Interior Decorators—which held its first conference with 342 charter members in Grand Rapids, Michigan, in July 1931. When the effects of the depression were being felt, the furniture industry found itself in particularly bad straits because it had depended so heavily on department store furniture buyers for its support. Two factory owners, Frank W. Mueller, the president of the Grand Rapids Furniture Manufacturing Association, and Joseph H. Brewer, the president of the Grand Rapids Convention Bureau, Inc., and Eric W. Dahl, the manager of the Grand Rapids Convention Bureau, Inc., invited interior decorators to attend a conference in Grand Rapids in order to form a national organization. It was observed that many of the decorators' clients were immune to, or at least less affected than the average American by, the depression. These were wealthy individuals and corporations who continued to make and spend money even during the worst of times, and Rorimer-Brooks owed its continued success to such clientele. Yet Rorimer believed that even in the worst times "people who really love beautiful things for their own sake will somehow find ways of continuing to enjoy them."[42]

The resulting new organization had its first national headquarters in Chicago until 1933, when it moved to New York. The Ohio chapter was formed in November of 1931 at Rorimer-Brooks Studios, just two months after Rorimer helped to charter the national organization. Rorimer was elected as the Ohio member of the Board of Governors, and Ray Irvin, vice-president of Rorimer-Brooks, was elected president of the Ohio chapter. In 1936 the name was changed to the American Institute of Decorators. Active membership required at least five years of training and experience, and fellowship status called for at least fifteen years in one's own business plus evidence of distinguished service to the profession and the Institute. Rorimer became its second national vice-president in 1932 and served until 1934.[43]

Long before the American Institute of Decorators made the distinction between a "decorator" and "designer," Rorimer recognized them as being different. His employees who carried out the planning, drafting, and rendering of interiors and furnishings were called designers, whereas his salesmen who met with clients to select and arrange furniture and accessories were decorators. In

1931 a decorator was defined by the American Institute of Decorators as "one who, by training and experience, is qualified to plan, design, and execute interiors and their furnishings and to supervise the various arts and crafts essential to their completion."[44] In reality, decorators were usually salesmen who mediated between the client and the firm, and it was the designer who more closely satisfied the requirements of the above definition. The term *designer* did not replace the term *decorator* until 1961 when the American Institute of Decorators changed its name to the American Institute of Designers.

In 1975 the American Institute of Designers merged with the National Society of Interior Designers to form the American Society of Interior Designers (ASID). Thus it was forty-four years after the original definition was formed that the American Society of Interior Designers expanded it to fit a changed society. Designers must be capable of working with or in place of the architect, who had traditionally designed and furnished the interior space of a building. Decorators select and purchase items such as floor and wall coverings and furniture, and they do not necessarily have artistic or design ability or training.

Rorimer knew this distinction long before it was articulated by the national organization for professional interior designers. He worked closely with architects, was formally trained to understand architecture, and helped design his own home in 1927. (When the Munich Kunstgewerbeschule honored Rorimer with a certificate on November 2, 1899, his title was Interior Architect.)[45] When Rorimer executed an interior design, it was complete and his shops were capable of producing it from the drafting table to its final installation. Rorimer's designers were qualified both by education and experience to analyze, plan, invent, and execute a new solution to each problem. Rorimer specialized in custom-made furnishings because he believed that each job was special. His leadership in the American Institute of Decorators would have been equally regarded by the American Society of Interior Designers in the more technological and complex world to come. Rorimer was a pioneer in his role as an interior designer.

Rorimer also played a pioneering role in introducing modern interior design and furnishings to America. If a single event spearheaded the spread of modernism in the decorative arts, it was L'Exposition des Arts Décoratifs et Industriels Modernes (Paris Exposition) held in Paris in the summer of 1925. The prevailing style of the exhibits was Art Moderne, which in the 1960s was labeled Art Deco. Although the French dominated the exhibition, many other nations were well represented, including Great Britain, Austria, Italy, the Netherlands, Sweden, Monaco, Czechoslovakia, U.S.S.R., and others. The United States was noticeably absent—Secretary of Commerce Herbert Hoover had declined the French invitation to participate because he saw no modern art in the United States at that time.[46] Instead, in February of 1925 Hoover appointed a three-person commission headed by the president of the American Association of Museums, Charles R. Richards, which in turn nominated 141 delegates to go to Paris and report on their findings. Rorimer was one of these nominees and one of the 108 delegates to arrive in Paris. He represented the

Association of Arts and Industries and was one of three "decorators" chosen to study and report specifically on interior design. Among the other delegates was Rorimer's friend Richard F. Bach of the Metropolitan Museum of Art.[47]

The commissioners and delegates attended the exposition from June 20 to July 4 when they were to be officially received and lavishly entertained by the French government. According to the *Report by the Commission,* "They were also given many exceptional opportunities to visit industrial establishments and buildings and apartments erected and furnished in the modern taste." Most of their time, however, was spent studying displays at this unique exposition. It was the first international exposition limited to the field of applied art, distinct from either fine art or manufactured goods. It was also the first to include only modern works—none was based on historic styles.[48]

Rorimer and the delegates from trade organizations representing industrial art fields were expected to make an official report on features of the exposition that were of interest to American manufacturers.[49] It was the commerce department whose special interests were to be the focus of both the observations and the written report. Rorimer was more than a decorator with an artistic eye. He was as talented in affairs of business as he was in art, and his recommendations to American manufacturers of home furnishings and industrial arts were well received.

When interviewed by the *Country Club News* while in Paris during the exposition, Rorimer explained its meaning. He began by observing that the European Art Moderne style that culminated at the Paris Exposition had taken decades to evolve. A relatively small exhibition that had been held in Darmstadt, Germany, in 1906 had represented the most extreme in modern design at the time. Rorimer explained that by 1925 the European public had realized that the Modern movement was more than an odd mutation in the evolution of Western art—indeed, it was the design product of everything that had preceded it. He went on to point out that modernism was a new look to old forms. Classicism of the distant past plus more recent historic events such as Art Nouveau and Arts and Crafts contributed to the unique look of Art Moderne as seen at the Exposition in 1925. Europe again claimed the front line of avantgarde design whereas, in Rorimer's words, "our own public has been slow to receive these fresh, very emphatic ideas. In the United States it has been easier to copy than to create."[50]

Not only were governmentally appointed delegates present at the Paris Exposition, but American designers and manufacturers took in the sights, and many returned home with new ideas and newly purchased designs and objects. Major museums, such as the Metropolitan Museum of Art, held exhibitions of modern decorative arts selected from the Paris Exposition, which introduced French Art Moderne designs to an often surprised public. Other cities hosting this exhibition, which was arranged by Charles Richards, included Boston, Chicago, Cleveland, Detroit, Minneapolis, Philadelphia, Pittsburgh, and St. Louis. One reviewer wrote of this exhibit, "It may be doubted if the works of art comprising the present exhibition receive generally the approbation they deserve. The exhibits will be entirely unfamiliar in style to the great majority of those who see them, and every student of the history of art knows that the unfamiliar meets at first with indifference, even with hostility."[51]

Perhaps the indifference to many of the exhibits at the Paris Exposition was not totally unfair, and even Rorimer admitted their shortcomings. When he returned home, Rorimer prepared a talk to be presented at the Cleveland Museum of Art. After he and Frary reviewed photographs of the exposition, Rorimer admitted, "Well, I suppose eighty-five per cent of the things shown were rather bad, many of them very bad; perhaps fifteen per cent were very good. . . . But that is a pretty good average for a new movement."[52] The past may seem golden because only a small proportion of really fine work has withstood the changing tastes through the years and has survived.

The modern French Exposition designs soon became more familiar to the American public when large department stores, such as Lord and Taylor and Macy's in New York, created displays.[53] Modernist architect and AUDAC member William E. Lescaze, who designed the modern exhibits at Loeser's Department Store in Brooklyn, wrote to Rorimer commending him on his modern designs:

Let me quote from a letter I have just received:—"Although no one in New England has enough nerve to build a really modern home, we have some grand examples of 'modernistic' stuff, but only one good piece of modern, the [Boston] Hotel Statler bar." I was delighted to read that, to think I knew the man who had done it, and thought it was too good to keep to myself ![54]

Yet even in New York, relatively few people were willing to accept the styling of this French import, and even fewer could afford to buy it.[55] Rorimer had personally felt the resistance to change in his own Cleveland clientele at a much earlier date and regretted the absence of demand for his most modern designs. It was the Paris Exposition that revived his optimism and assured him that America would soon discover its own modern movement. While still in Paris in 1925, he said, "It is therefore safe to predict that changes—perhaps very sweeping changes—are near at hand in the fields of American architecture, in household furnishings and in clothing—for the raiment of the people is subtly affected by the general styles in architecture and applied art." Rorimer's participation at the Paris Exposition would contribute to those "very sweeping changes" that would soon occur across America. "The New Movement in art is like a seismic disturbance—it registers simultaneously throughout the world," he said.[56] If Americans would become less resistant to modernism, then Rorimer saw a chance to participate in the move toward a modern American style.

When interviewed by the *New York Times* upon his return from Paris, Rorimer was both displeased with the state of design in America and hopeful about its future. He said, "America has never been able to contribute much originality to the decorative arts. . . . Even the early American specimens, so much in vogue now, were direct adaptations of European models. . . . Never-theless, in spite of the fact that we are still largely copyists, our designers have made great strides in the last fifteen years and a trend toward originality is breaking through the old habits of accepting everything European."[57]

French Art Moderne (Art Deco) was not popular in America partly because of its high cost and also because American designers were struggling to de-velop a native style. During the next fifteen years American designers at last broke loose of the hold that Europe had had on them for three centuries. Particularly in the field of industrial design, America finally achieved an inter-national position. In the decorative arts, dominated by furniture, there devel-oped an original and distinct style inspired by French Art Moderne but appropriately American, variously called Thirties Modern, Depression Mod-ern, Streamlined Modern, Zig-Zag Modern, or incorrectly, Art Deco. The term *Art Deco* is usually inappropriate for this modern American style because, ac-cording to Martin Greif, "True Deco had been soft, preferring lavish curves and curlicues in hand-wrought ballustrades and flower-patterned metal grill-work. But the modernistic was hard and largely angular." The style called "Modern" in the 1930s and later called Depression Modern was clean, unclut-tered, and innocent. Its objectives were efficiency, economy, and right appear-ance. Americans during the depression "adopted simple forms not as an escape from its complex age, but, rather as a celebration of it."[58] Rorimer was one of the many designers to experiment with this new idiom. Although such furniture was usually mass-produced, Rorimer continued to make his individ-ually because of his regard for fine craftsmanship.

In the search for an American identity in modern decorative arts, design was an important part of Rorimer's observations and wishes, but he also con-tinued to campaign for the Arts and Crafts ideal of good workmanship and quality. After returning from the Paris Exposition he pointed out:

> Our greatest problem is the lack of draftsmanship among our artisans. In Europe every child who is to become a carpenter, an iron worker, or a maker of furniture is grounded from infancy in drawing and modeling. The consequence is that those who have exceptional ability have a chance to develop it and even the clum-siest artisan gets some conception of contour. This lack of imaginative training in our workmen is, of course, due to our American passion for quantity production, and we shall never get very far until individual craftsmanship comes in for some share of appreciation. But here again are some signs that we are beginning to see the light. I hope for much in the way of stimulation to the American arts from the Paris Exposition.[59]

Curiously, America, in searching for its identity in the applied arts, again looked toward Europe for its lead, this time for quality of construction as well as of design. But an unforeseen event prevented this from being realized on a large scale. The realities of the depression led designers, manufacturers, and consumers to choose a different path than they might have chosen had better

34

times prevailed. America did break out of the copyist syndrome, but economy and quantity were high on the list of priorities.

Rorimer's participation in America's move toward modernism did not (with a few exceptions) include mass production. His concerns were for styling and fine construction, and although most American modern furniture was mass-produced, Rorimer-Brooks continued its tradition of custom making its designs. This may help to explain the lack of recognition Rorimer received, even though he designed and produced sophisticated modern pieces. When Rorimer built furniture for his own home, it was modern.[60]

His participation in AUDAC, an organization striving to advance modern design in America, and in the American Institute of Decorators, an organization striving to modernize the field of interior design, confirms Rorimer's commitment to modernization. Other involvements, such as with the Cleveland School of Art and the Cleveland Museum of Art, demonstrate his general commitment to art and its history.

Rorimer consciously borrowed from history to create fresh designs suited to a technological society. He reused old designs without altering them at the same time that he created totally new forms with little or no apparent historical precedent. According to Frary, who had worked beside Rorimer: "He drew the acanthus with all the skill and knowledge of the Greek sculptor, but he returned from his studies with a boyish enthusiasm for the new movement in design that was then making itself felt in the schools abroad. He never lost that urge to forge ahead in thought. . . . He kept ever in step with progress, and was alert to see what was worth while in the new."[61] Rorimer was not a traditionalist, but a versatile modernist versed in the use of traditional forms. His oeuvre included whatever suited his taste and his clients' needs. Rorimer's basic philosophy was modern, and he was skilled at creating innovative, if not future-oriented, designs. The issue of modern versus traditional was of great interest during his lifetime and was a recurring theme throughout his career. After unsuccessful attempts at introducing modern interiors to Cleveland, Rorimer realized that the majority of his work would have to be traditional. Yet he continued to experiment and to produce modern designs.

⤙ 3 ⤚

THE COMPANY

While Rorimer was growing up in the 1870s and 1880s America had few interior design firms. Among the first to specialize in interior design and cater to an East Coast elite was Herter Brothers, a leading New York cabinetmaking and decorating firm active from the mid-1860s to 1882. The two German-born brothers, Gustav and Christian Herter, departed from the typical historical revivals of the period and worked in the Eastlake style with a Japanese flavor. All Herter pieces were expensive, making lavish use of inlay, ebonizing, and carving, always of the finest craftsmanship.[1]

One of the earliest American firms to focus on decorative art and interior decoration was Associated Artists, formed in 1879 by a partnership between Louis Comfort Tiffany, Samuel Colman, Lockwood de Forest, and Candace Wheeler.[2] Each partner was in charge of a specific department: Tiffany worked in glass, Wheeler in textiles and embroidery, de Forest in carving and wood decoration, and Colman with color. They had all traveled extensively, which enhanced their contributions to the firm. According to historian Wilson Faude, "Each interior by Associated Artists was unique, yet all were consistent with the firm's philosophy of beauty, color, harmony, function, and appropriateness to the owner." By the 1880s Associated Artists was becoming one of New York's top decorating concerns.[3]

Much of Associated Artists' work came to them from the architectural firm of McKim, Mead and White. Important clients included Ogden Goelet, Cornelius Vanderbilt II, Hamilton Fish, J. Taylor Johnson, and the White House. The style was still High Victorian but represented the Aesthetic movement in America with exotic elements such as Islamic carvings, embroidered hangings, painted friezes, and colored glass. Incorporating exotic elements into their product, working with architects, and catering to a wealthy clientele were features common to both Associated Artists and Rorimer-Brooks.

Associated Artists was a short-lived partnership that dissolved in 1883. Wheeler, who in 1877 had established the Society of Decorative Art to aid the cause of women's education, kept the name Associated Artists and continued to design textiles and wallpapers. According to Faude, "The variety and scope of Associated Artists' work under Candace Wheeler's direction was recognized and well received, and she herself gained the distinction of being America's foremost textile designer." Associated Artists under Wheeler lasted until 1907. From 1879 to 1907 Associated Artists tried to produce designs that represented the tastes of their time. In addition to breaking with the past they tried to break away from dependence on foreign influence and create American designs using mostly American materials.[4]

When Tiffany left the firm in 1883 he concentrated on his glassmaking, from which he earned his reputation and place in history as America's foremost practitioner in the Art Nouveau style. Stained glass windows and lamps and hand-blown Favrile glass objects were his mainstay, but Tiffany Studios included a decorating service that supplied "artistic furniture," "quality reproductions," and fabrics for draperies and bedspreads. In 1898 Tiffany Studios absorbed the Schmitt Brothers Furniture Company, which remained until 1907.[5]

Associated Artists, a versatile decorating firm, succumbed to the specializations preferred by its individual partners. After its brief attempt at becoming a full-service decorating company, it broke up into Wheeler's textile design business and Tiffany's glassmaking bonanza. Today the name of Louis Comfort Tiffany is rarely associated with his early partnership in a decorating firm. It is almost synonymous with stained glass windows and lamp shades and also with mouth-blown Art Nouveau glass vessels. In fact, the generic term *Tiffany shade* refers to various contemporary reproductions of colored leaded glass lamp shades regardless of manufacturing methods or company.

The architect Ogden Codman gained notoriety in the field of interior decorating after collaborating with novelist Edith Wharton in writing *The Decoration of Houses*. The book remains a classic in turn-of-the-century interior decoration.[6] In the early twentieth century, women without any formal design training began to enter the decorating field, such as Elsie de Wolfe, who is considered to be America's first professional woman decorator. De Wolfe borrowed ideas from France and England and stressed comfort and lightness in color and content from the turn of the century until after World War II. She popularized pastel colors, especially beige, and preferred Neoclassical styles. Ruby Ross Wood was a journalist and de Wolfe's first disciple. In 1918 she ran America's first known department store decorating service, called Au Quatrième, in Wanamaker's of New York, where she stressed comfortable, informal, English-style rooms. Nancy McClelland, the creator of Au Quatrième in 1913, graduated from Vassar College and studied art history while in Paris for six years. She created formal interiors in period styles. Rose Cumming worked briefly at Au Quatrième and then opened her own shop in 1921 with an emphasis on strong deep colors.[7]

In November of 1924 Eleanor McMillen Brown, who had graduated from the three-year design course at the New York School of Fine and Applied Arts, started her own company called McMillen, Inc. According to author

Erica Brown, "It is safe to say that McMillen, Inc. was the first professional full-service interior decorating firm in America."[8] Perhaps it was the first one run by a woman, since Rorimer-Brooks had already been in operation for a generation.

With the help of William Odom, head of the Paris branch of the New York School of Fine and Applied Arts, McMillen imported French and English eighteenth-century antiques. Rorimer also imported antiques that he personally selected during his trips to Europe. What characterized McMillen's style was its consistency and its conservatism. For sixty years French Neoclassicism was the preferred style. Even after the 1925 Paris Exposition McMillen was unaffected by the surrounding changes. In an interview with *Country Life* in 1929, Eleanor McMillen Brown expressed her dislike for the modern movement. According to Brown, even in the late 1930s, "Modernism in America was essentially the vernacular of architects. Decorators, who were now proliferating and being taken seriously as professionals, throughout the decade favored a much more romantic look, one that had its roots in tradition."[9] McMillen's conservatism and preoccupation with the past were comfortable and reassuring to her clientele. It was neither threatening nor exciting, both of which were qualities inherent in modern design.

In Cleveland, Rorimer, who was excited by modern design and had the ability to use it, was catering to the same type of clientele that patronized Mc-Millen, Inc. Rorimer served the taste of this group by manufacturing and selling fine antique reproduction furniture, which contributed to his success. However, unlike McMillen, with her narrow commitment to French Neoclassicism, Rorimer's antique-style repertoire spanned three centuries and embraced most of the Western world. Despite the fact that New York was America's most fertile center in the development of modern design, McMillen flourished for years in New York selling pink silk and white antiqued wood. If New Yorkers were this conservative, then what chance could Rorimer possibly have had to express himself in Cleveland? His compromise between modernism and the prevailing conservatism turned out to be the ideal formula for success at that time and in that place. An audience with limited expertise in art history allowed him to experiment with novel combinations of historic styles. To those expecting something more traditional, Rorimer's hybridizations were often more creative and unusual than his clients realized. The use of design features from multiple countries and centuries combined in one piece of furniture was typical of much of Rorimer's traditional work, and what often passed for familiar traditional furnishings was actually highly original and unique.

Rorimer-Brooks occupied a special niche in the design world and therefore suffered little from competition by similar firms. If it suffered at all, it was in the 1930s and for the same economic reasons affecting other businesses during the aftermath of the great stock market crash. Perhaps Rorimer-Brooks was not hit as hard as those companies that depended on various classes of people to buy their product. As long as there was an upper middle class in the Cleveland area, Rorimer-Brooks could survive the 1930s. Moreover, the Statler Hotel chain account gave Rorimer-Brooks the notoriety needed to win commissions beyond Cleveland and the business to maintain its cash flow during that economically precarious decade.

From the beginning Rorimer's success was partly due to his flexibility and ability to recognize opportunity. Rorimer had never intended to make interior design his life's work. His training and real love were for sculpting, whether modeling in clay and plaster or carving wood. His first attempts in business were to establish himself as a sculptor and designer of modeled interior ornamentations similar to what he exhibited at the Cleveland Architectural Club, but his efforts were fruitless in Cleveland near the turn of the century. Rorimer turned to making furniture out of the simple need to furnish his own studio, and he soon discovered that fine furniture was a very salable item. He designed and built furniture to earn a living, and he also designed stained glass windows, jewelry and silver objects, and he continued to sketch.[10]

Herman Matzen, who had taught Rorimer how to carve and sculpt at the Manual Training School and was later instrumental in securing his faculty position at the Cleveland School of Art, was credited by Rorimer with encouraging him to enter the newly developing field of interior design.[11] Rorimer's compromise enabled him to keep one foot in the world of art and sculpture and the other in the world of business—only the first artistic compromise Rorimer would make for the sake of economics. Happily, not only did the sculptural quality of his early furniture bring Rorimer artistic satisfaction, it pleased his clients. Demand for his hand-carved furniture, paneling, staircases, and other interior architecture brought Rorimer early recognition.

In 1896, after returning from Europe, Rorimer opened his first studio specializing in handmade furniture. It was located at 442 of the Old Arcade, a 400-foot-long structure connecting Euclid and Superior Avenues near Public Square in downtown Cleveland. Opened in 1890, the Arcade's five-story-high railed balconies beneath a glass roof earned it the name "Cleveland's crystal palace." M. James Bowman was Rorimer's partner for a short time, calling the studio Rohrheimer and Bowman. Nearby in the Arcade was the headquarters of the Cleveland Architectural Club, which had been organized two years earlier. Rorimer's first commission was a large high-backed carved oak bench for Clevelander Luther Allen. Rorimer was so enthusiastic that he embellished the piece with an inscription carved across the back, the quote from Keats, "A thing of beauty is a joy forever." Unfortunately, Mr. Allen did not appreciate Rorimer's added touch and refused to take delivery of the bench. Rorimer was heartbroken, so he put it in the basement of his studio where it remained for over thirty years. When Rorimer was made president of the Cleveland Playhouse in 1932, he resurrected his "thing of beauty" and placed it in the Playhouse lobby, where it stands today.[12] The quote from Keats continued to exemplify Rorimer's philosophy throughout his life.

In 1898 Rorimer acquired a new partner, Louis H. Hays, and moved to 901 of the Garfield Building in downtown Cleveland. Hays had several things in

40

common with Rorimer. His father Joseph, like Rorimer's, was an important early Jewish immigrant to Cleveland. Hays was about the same age as Rorimer, one year younger, and they were friends. Both were married while working as partners—Hays to Jessie Feiss in 1902 and Rorimer to Edith Joseph in 1903. Rorimer had met Edith in 1901 while designing the Cincinnati home of her father, Joseph Joseph, who was prominent in the iron and steel business. Joseph died the year after Edith's marriage to Rorimer, leaving eleven children and a widow, who lived to the age of 96.[13]

By 1900 Rohrheimer and Hays had shops at 154–58 Champlain Street and studios at a separate address, 901–5 in the Garfield Building. At this early date the shops were well equipped, as seen in contemporary photographs. The partnership lasted until 1904, when Hays left the decorating business to form the Federal Knitting Company.[14] Rorimer then moved to 277–85 Old Erie Street near Euclid Avenue, and his first important commission was the decoration and furnishing of the Chamber of Commerce clubrooms in downtown Cleveland.[15] From 1905 until 1910 Rorimer had no partners and changed his name to Rorheimer by dropping the *h*. Then in 1910 the name Rorheimer-Brooks first appeared when Rorimer merged with Cleveland's oldest interior decorating firm, the Brooks Household Art Company.

The first appearance of the Brooks Household Art Company in the *Cleveland City Directory* was in 1886, although it had been established in the mid-nineteenth century in Buffalo, New York. In 1889 Brooks-Otis Household Art Company was at 53 Euclid Avenue, with Brooks as its president and manager in partnership with William L. Otis. Brooks-Otis continued until 1893 when Otis left and Brooks took Frederick W. Day as its secretary. Ihna Thayer Frary, Rorimer's friend since they attended the Manual Training School together, was chief designer at Brooks Household Art Company from 1894 to 1909. He joined Rorimer-Brooks briefly and later became the membership and publicity secretary for the Cleveland Museum of Art and published books on Ohio architecture.[16]

By 1904 there were five names of interior decorating firms listed in Cleveland: Brooks, Rohrheimer and Hays, Otis (formerly of Brooks-Otis), Bowman (not formerly of Rohrheimer and Bowman), and one other.[17] Few Clevelanders, in fact few Americans outside of New York, had recognized a need to employ trained interior designers as professionals related to, but separate from, architects and builders. Interior design as a profession would not become well established for decades. Rorimer had entered the field at a time when Cleveland was enjoying increased prosperity. Migrations to suburbs such as Shaker Heights and Cleveland Heights were beginning, and with the increased population came countless homes requiring fashionable interiors. Magazines promoted home beautification, and travel opportunities helped to educate a new generation of homeowners, many of whom would display Rorimer-Brooks interiors.

Before taking on Brooks, Rorheimer Studios moved to 1907–31 East Ninth Street. There Rorimer personally carved an ornate staircase that was later

Preparing lumber at Rohrheimer and Hays shops on Champlain Street, Cleveland, in 1900. *Courtesy of the Rorimer family.*

installed at his permanent location, the building at 2232 Euclid Avenue which he had built. The staircase still stands, but with the unfortunate addition of several coats of paint.

Rorimer had worked briefly as a woodcarver for Brooks-Otis before leaving for Europe to study, so he was well acquainted with both Edward Brooks and the firm.[18] They specialized in antique furniture and reproductions, mantels, interior woodwork, draperies, and other interior decoration. Brooks kept little or no furniture on hand, because everything was made to order, whether an original design or an antique reproduction. Brooks used almost no machinery—everything was made by hand of the finest materials. "If we make a piece of furniture for you, we are careful not to duplicate it in your own city or immediate neighborhood," they claimed in *The House Beautiful.* Exclusivity was built into the item's manufacture and its cost, which limited the number of potential customers. Yet Brooks Household Art Company was considered to be

42

Cabinet shop at Rohrheimer and Hays, Champlain Street, Cleveland, in 1900.
Courtesy of the Rorimer family.

one of the foremost decorating establishments in America, with some of its
important work being done outside of Cleveland.[19]

When Brooks was experiencing financial difficulties in about 1910, Rorimer
saw it as an opportunity to merge. He could eliminate his biggest competitor
by the merger and gain a respected name and an established clientele. In addition, the Brooks name helped to anglicize the sound of Rorheimer, which
was legally changed to Rorimer in 1917. In 1911 Rorimer-Brooks was considered to be the largest institution of its kind west of New York, employing over
one hundred skilled workers.[20]

In 1916 Rorimer-Brooks moved to their newly constructed 2232 Euclid Avenue building, and by 1917 the firm had stopped changing partners, addresses, and the spelling of its name. Since Brooks had been in the process of
retiring when he merged with Rorimer, the name Rorimer-Brooks was only
titular. Rorimer was the only company head until he died in 1939. The name

Carving shop, Rohrheimer and Hays, Champlain Street, Cleveland, in 1900. *Courtesy of the Rorimer family.*-

Rorimer-Brooks, Inc., was then used by former employees until 1957, when they closed the doors at 2232 Euclid Avenue.

Of the many years that the company was in operation, the 1920s and early 1930s were probably the most colorful. Judging by the number of full-page advertisements in Cleveland periodicals during the late 1920s and early 1930s, these were also prosperous years for Rorimer-Brooks.[21] After returning home from the 1925 Paris Exposition, Rorimer's interest in Art Moderne intensified. In 1930 he ran an advertisement in the local periodical *Your Garden* and pictured an Art Moderne console table and mirror that were also featured in a seven-page article about Rorimer in the December 14, 1929, issue of the *Cleveland Bystander.*[22] Use of words like "unusual," "individuality," and "distinction" in the text of the advertisement suggests that these pieces were not intended

44

Another view of carving shop, Rohrheimer and Hays, Champlain Street, Cleveland, in 1900. *Courtesy of the Rorimer family.*

for everyone. Yet Rorimer must have felt that by 1930 at least some Clevelanders would begin to accept these extreme modern designs.

The Rorimer-Brooks advertisement in the Cleveland Orchestra special concert program—dated February 5–7, 1931, for the dedication of Severence Hall—pictures another modern piece, also from the 1929 *Bystander* article. But

Casting plaster moldings at the Champlain Street shops, Rohrheimer and Hays, Cleveland, in 1900. *Courtesy of the Rorimer family.*

the great majority of illustrated advertisements for Rorimer-Brooks in Cleveland periodicals pictured more traditional antique or antique reproduction pieces. Typical examples can be found in the February 1932 advertisement in *Your Garden and Home*. William and Mary and Queen Anne antique reproductions, as well as other Colonial Revival styles, were indicative of prevailing

46

Possibly the leather-working shop at Rohrheimer and Hays on Champlain Street, Cleveland, in 1900. *Courtesy of the Rorimer family.*

tastes to which Rorimer-Brooks catered. One advertisement read, "Styles come and go, but through the years the furnishings of the Georgian period—with their rich simplicity and purity of design—always endure." In another 1929 advertisement, it was noted that Duncan Phyfe *"and many other fine examples of early American furniture and furnishings can be seen in our Studios or can be reproduced in our shops."* It is clear that Rorimer-Brooks promoted historic styles in its advertisements and that there was a reliable market for this type of furniture. But Rorimer-Brooks did not create this demand as much as it satisfied it. The popularity of traditional furnishings was widespread, as indicated in a furniture history book published by the Century Furniture Company of Grand Rapids, Michigan. Most of the photographs of "period" furniture that accompanied the text had been recently manufactured by the company, which claimed: "Today, the better pieces of furniture may be reproductions of the earlier masterpieces, or they may be intelligent modern adaptations of certain

47

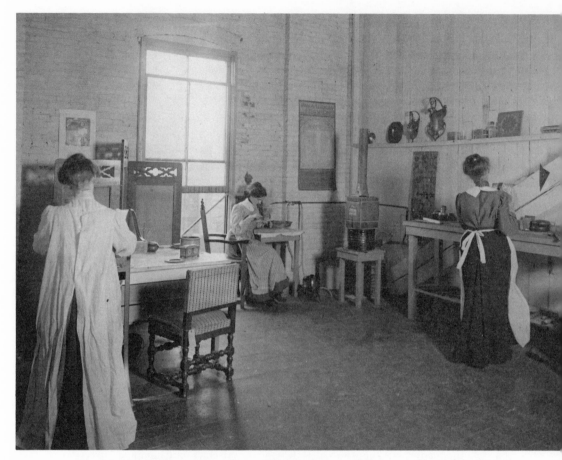

Possibly the leather-tooling shop of Rohrheimer and Hays on Champlain Street, Cleveland, in 1900. *Courtesy of the Rorimer family.*

historic styles. . . . Modern furniture draws its inspiration liberally from the past and adds the ingenuity of modern craftsmanship and modern machinery."[23]

Not all of Rorimer-Brooks's antique reproductions were meant to be accurate, and none were intended to deceive. An advertisement in *Your Garden* in March 1930 picturing a seventeenth-century-style court cupboard reads, "The unusually fine Court Cupboard illustrated is the product of our own shops built from designs by our own artists."[24] Some of these antique reproductions were true copies of original pieces, while others were versions created in the shop. In order to produce a version of an historic piece, the designer and craftsmen needed to have a thorough understanding of both historic style and manufacturing techniques. The execution of these new versions of old furniture entailed the use of modern methods in varying degrees. When real

48

Gold leafing, Rohrheimer and Hays, Champlain Street, Cleveland, in 1900. *Courtesy of the Rorimer family.*

accuracy was a goal, even the wood was antique, and recycled parts from old pieces were sometimes used. In most cases, however, only stylistic features were borrowed.

In addition to manufacturing pieces based on historic American or European designs in its own shops, Rorimer-Brooks also had designs executed in Europe by European craftsmen. For example, one 1931 advertisement read: "The gayly colored base of this exquisite lamp was hand painted in Italy especially for Rorimer-Brooks. The shade, too, was hand painted. It is one of a group of Italian vase lamps, each one an exclusive, individual design." While Rorimer-Brooks's advertisements pictured examples of furniture and accessories both designed and manufactured at their studios or imported from Europe, the emphasis was on products of their own shops. Rorimer-Brooks was not only proud of its products but also of the shops in which they were made. This is illustrated by a Christmas advertisement in *Your Garden and Home*

49

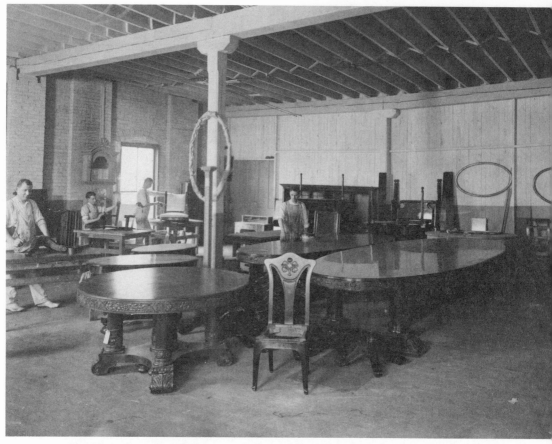

Finishing shop, Rohrheimer and Hays, Champlain Street, Cleveland, in 1900.
Courtesy of the Rorimer family.

for 1931, which pictures staff members at work in the upholstery and the
drapery rooms.[25]

The structure housing this department was on Prospect Avenue and was
connected to the main cabinet shop by a covered catwalk. Other contemporary
photographs of shops in the 1920s include the cabinet shop, carving studio,
and finishing room. In the cabinet shop, Frank Reicheldt (assistant to Fred
Wittmus, the Cleveland May Show winner in the early 1920s) is pictured second from the left (see page 54). In the photo of the wood-carvers, master
wood-carver John Nepodal is the first man on the left (see page 55). The
finishing room was an L-shaped room on the third floor of the building, and
it was headed by Vorn Lielser. Michele "Mike" Carome, a master finisher working under Lielser, is pictured in the foreground with the table (see page 56).
Carome was born in Italy in 1892 and came to Cleveland in 1894, settling in
Little Italy near University Circle. He began as a furniture refinisher at

Upholstery shop, Rohrheimer and Hays, Champlain Street, Cleveland, in 1900.
Courtesy of the Rorimer family.

Rorimer-Brooks in the early 1910s and later specialized in interior painting, gold leafing, and marbleizing.[26]

Advertisements are a good indication of what the company valued and promoted. Rorimer-Brooks's self-image and its perception of its public image can be understood by the careful wording and selection of items for illustrations. "Decorators," "importers," and "manufacturers" were the terms most commonly used to describe the firm. The advertisements featured fabrics, rugs, authentic reproductions, antiques, and wood interiors. Rorimer-Brooks never hesitated to picture an impressive job, such as the Greenbrier Resort in White Sulphur Springs, West Virginia. When its short-lived branch at 13231 Shaker Square was advertised, the audience was informed that it was next door to the Shaker Tavern, which had been decorated and furnished by the company.

Drapery shop, Rohrheimer and Hays, Champlain Street, Cleveland, in 1900. *Courtesy of the Rorimer family.*

Quality was of such importance that a special Rorimer-Brooks furniture cleaner was developed. ("To keep your furniture in perfect condition use the 'R. B.' furniture cleaner prepared especially for use on the finest furniture. One dollar a bottle.")[27]

Quality was one way Rorimer-Brooks kept its clientele, because the company depended on return customers at least as much as on attracting new ones. One itemized list of purchases made by Dr. R. W. Scott of Shaker Heights from 1935 to 1937 includes sixty items, sets (such as chairs), and services totaling $4,592.33. For example, a sideboard cost $283, a leather arm chair $115, and a glass cabinet lowered from its original height cost $21. Names of many other individual clients are found in a small handwritten "Shop Detail Book" that focuses on the 1930s. From this document it is clear that many clients did

Drapery shop, Rorimer-Brooks, 2232 Euclid Avenue, Cleveland, 1920s. *Courtesy of the Rorimer family.*

return to Rorimer-Brooks again and again (see appendix A for this list). In addition to clients, the book includes names of designers and salesmen (decorators). Designers worked at the shops and did not usually go out to meet clients. That role was left to the salesmen, who acted as intermediaries between client and designer.[28]

In addition to identifying employees, the "Shop Detail Book" indicates when they were active in the company and who their clients were. For example, salesmen Herbert Cave, Robert Boone, and Phillip T. Hummel were among the last entries in the book at the end of 1938. They were three of the partners who took over the firm when Rorimer died one year later. Louis Rorimer also appears until the end, so his fatal illness must have been relatively brief. The

Cabinet shop with Mr. Kircher *(left)* and Frank Reicheldt *(second from left)*, Rorimer-Brooks, 2232 Euclid Avenue, Cleveland, 1920s. *Courtesy of the Rorimer family.*

"Shop Detail Book" demonstrates that Rorimer personally attended to the Statler accounts in at least six different cities. His interest in the Statlers went beyond their interior decoration and furnishing. As a member of the board of directors and substantial stockholder in the Statler Corporation, he cared about that company as well as about his own.

Ray Irvin's initials do not appear in the "Shop Detail Book" later than December of 1933, because this is when he left to form his own decorating business. Irvin and Company became Rorimer-Brooks's competitor when Irvin resigned as vice-president and opened a company at Shaker Square. Later, in 1957 when Rorimer-Brooks finally closed, there was an informal merger with Irvin and Company, and several of its employees, such as Phil Hummel, stayed

Carving shop with John Nepodal *(left)*, Rorimer-Brooks, 2232 Euclid Avenue, Cleveland, 1920s. *Courtesy of the Rorimer family.*

on. It was at this time that Irvin and Company disposed of the illustrated Rorimer-Brooks records. Sixty years of company records must have been cumbersome indeed, but those who had been at Rorimer-Brooks were furious when no one even bothered to save the large folio of furniture photographs representing every design ever made at Rorimer-Brooks. Irvin and Company remained in business for another nineteen years until it closed its doors at Shaker Square in 1976.[29]

Employees in the "Shop Detail Book" who have been identified include George Francis Adamadis, Mr. Westrack, chief designer William B. Green, Andrew E. Probala, who became chief designer after Green, William Ahearn, Lou Caldwill, and Howard Brook Pierce. Most of the information contained in the

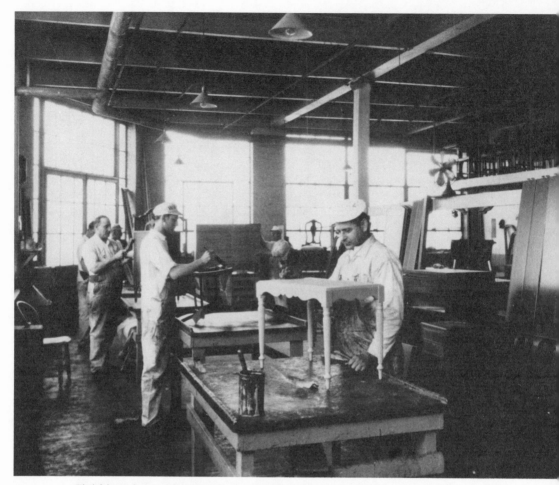

Finishing shop with Mike Carome *(right)*, Rorimer-Brooks, 2232 Euclid Avenue, Cleveland, 1920s. *Courtesy of the Rorimer family.*

"Shop Detail Book" pertains to dates. Because the entries are in chronological order, the time of employees' activity with the company can be approximated. Clients and specific orders can be identified, as well as the frequency of clients' visits. The dates of introduction and continued use of new designs can also be seen for the decade covered in the book.

Additional employee information is available only for 1938 and 1939. According to payroll ledger sheets for these years, the number of factory workers, which included cabinetmakers, finishers, upholsterers, and other craftsmen, fluctuated weekly. The number ranged from nineteen to thirty-eight and the most sizable fluctuations (between five and sixteen) occurred within the finishers category. These changes in employee numbers followed no obvious seasonal pattern. Nor was there a relationship between the fluctuations in individual crafts, such as between cabinetmakers and finishers. Prior to 1938, additional part-time craftsmen were frequently needed, especially when Rorimer would suddenly bring in a large order, such as from one of the Statler Hotels. The later (1938–39) fluctuations in staff numbers were certainly caused by similar increases and decreases in orders. Because finishing work is particularly time consuming, there would have been a greater need for extra temporary finishers, especially when there was a deadline to meet.[30]

One conclusion based on the payroll sheets that can be made about the furniture produced in 1938 and 1939 is that little carving was done. Prior to the 1930s carving had been a major feature of furniture and interior architecture made by Rorimer-Brooks and a large staff of carvers had been employed.[31] Only one part-time wood-carver was listed for 1938 and 1939. Styles had changed, and the cleaner lines of the 1930s provided few employment opportunities for wood-carvers, a trend that has not since reversed.

Besides factory workers, the other employee category found on the payroll sheets was office, which included designers and salesmen as well as clerical workers. This group was more stable than the factory, and it ranged from between nineteen and twenty-four employees in 1938 and 1939. The two designers and nine salesmen remained fairly constant throughout the period.

The largest variations found on the payroll sheets are in employee salaries. Rorimer's recorded $9,000 salary in 1938 was more than seven times the amount earned by the average American worker in that year, although it represented only a portion of his total income.[32] Copies of Rorimer's Federal Income Tax 1040 forms dated 1914 and 1919 indicate that his salary was a relatively small portion of his total income in those years, and probably in 1938 as well. In 1914 Rorimer's salary was $15,000 out of a total declared income of $56,000, when the average annual salary of a worker in wholesale and retail trade was $706. Rorimer's 1919 salary was $25,000 out of a total declared income of nearly $60,000. In that year the average wage for workers in wholesale and retail trade was $1,070.[33] On an undated 1040 form his salary was $15,000, and the total declared income was $71,000, indicating that salary and income increases were not necessarily proportionate. One obvious conclusion that can be made is that Rorimer-Brooks was successful and extremely lucrative for Rorimer. His substantial personal income financed extensive traveling and collecting, luxuries enjoyed by few other Americans at that time.

The average American worker earned $1,230 in 1938. Salaries in manufacturing ($1,296) and wholesale-retail trade ($1,352) were higher than the national average for all workers. The 1939 median wage for male craftsmen and foremen was $1,309, whereas the median for females wad $827. Many of Rorimer's employees earned much more than the national average for similar professions. Three of the company's top men—William H. Webster (first vice-president since 1915), Robert A. Boone, and Herbert F. Cave—earned $4,200, $3,432 and $4,004 respectively in 1938, about triple the national average. Decorator Philip T. Hummel earned $2,600, and craftsmen Frank Reicheldt and

Louis Rorimer touching up woodwork in a back storeroom of Rorimer-Brooks Studios, 2232 Euclid Avenue, 1920s. *Courtesy of the Rorimer family.*

Ulrich Leber, at $2,080 and $2,735, earned about double the national average. On the other hand, annual wages of the young and inexperienced decorators, James W. Akeroyd and Louise C. Thompson were close to the national average, and several other employees who earned between $800 and $1,000 were paid a relatively low wage.[34]

On the whole, Rorimer-Brooks employees earned good salaries for their professions in 1938. Several employees had been with the company for many years. For example, Leber, who had worked on the May Show exhibits in 1919, and Reicheldt had already been at Rorimer-Brooks for some time. Hummel joined the company in 1928, remained until the merger with Irvin and Company in 1957, then joined Irvin and Company. According to Andrew Probala, it was common for employees to remain with Rorimer-Brooks for decades.[35] Salaries would have been one incentive to stay, and it is reasonable to assume that employees had always earned fair wages.

Rorimer was a generous man, especially with his time and knowledge. He was also a keen businessman and was known to get the most for his money. Besides traveling to Europe, Rorimer made frequent trips to New York, where he was involved in organizations and business and kept up with the latest trends. When he learned that one of his young designers, Andrew Probala, had not seen the fine buildings of New York, he handed Probala a check for $100 and told him to take a train and spend a week absorbing as much as he could. Probala had never seen that much money at one time, and he purchased a regular ticket, rather than one for the more expensive sleeping car. He sat up all night on the train, arrived in New York the next day exhausted, and checked into the cheapest hotel he could find. Two meals a day and long walks to save cab fare enabled Probala to stretch his week in New York to fifteen days. When he finally returned to Cleveland, Rorimer asked what had happened, since he had given him funds for only a one week stay. When Probala explained that he was able to save money by living without a few comforts, Rorimer exclaimed, "Oh, Andy, next time you'll have to go to New York with me—and teach me how to do it!" Probala did return there with Rorimer, as well as travel with him to other cities, and he said that Rorimer was really a very enjoyable traveling companion.[36]

The attraction of working for Rorimer-Brooks was not only the pay, but also the opportunity to make use of one's training and experience and to learn more. In letters written to Rorimer by decorators and designers seeking jobs, the starting salary was not an issue. Several of those seeking positions with the company had been trained in Europe and/or had worked in Europe. Some had worked for important New York designers, such as modernists Eugene Schoen and Gilbert Rohde, and one applicant was the brother-in-law of Bauhaus instructor and artist Joseph Albers.[37] If designers from New York and Chicago were eager to relocate in Cleveland to join Rorimer-Brooks, then the attraction must have been strong.

Employees regarded Rorimer as a teacher, and he always rewarded excellence with praise and encouragement. Financial renumeration was sometimes another matter, for Rorimer tried not to pay more than what was absolutely necessary. He may have lost some good people because of his reluctance to negotiate higher salaries. For example, when William Green died, Andrew Probala was made the new chief designer. After being given more and more responsibility and working long hours, sometimes well into the night, without overtime pay (except thirty-five cents for dinner), Probala requested a higher salary. "Why, I can go to New York and bring back two designers for what you're asking," Rorimer replied. "Mr. Rorimer," answered Probala, "I was about to give you a month's notice, but since you can replace me so easily, I need only give you two weeks." During the two weeks, Rorimer did go to New

York, but found that designers were earning even more there than they were in Cleveland. He returned, said nothing, but waited for the two weeks to pass. Rorimer knew that Probala would come into the studio on Saturday to collect his things, so he waited until the last moment and said, "All right, Andy, I'll call your bluff and give you what you requested." "I'm not bluffing, Mr. Rorimer, I'm leaving," said Probala. He did leave, and his new salary with another firm was comparable to what Rorimer would have paid him. Later Rorimer offered to double Probala's original pay if he would return to Rorimer-Brooks, but the two never worked together again, although they remained friends.[38]

Salesmen's salaries do not appear to reflect commissions, because the highest paid salesmen did not necessarily sell the most merchandise. According to a single incomplete preliminary sales report sheet dated 1938, there were $230,038 in sales. It is not clear what this figure means—whether it is a gross or a net amount, the time period covered, and whether the figure represents one or more categories of sales. It is clear, however, that Rorimer sold the most merchandise, followed by Boone, Hummel, Cave, and Thompson. According to the United States Board of Tax Appeals, Rorimer-Brooks's net income was $52,000 in 1926, jumped to $279,000 in 1927, and dropped to $207,000 in 1928. These are the only figures available for those years.[39]

Individual monthly salesmen's record sheets from January 1939 through March 1940 indicate that the 1938 summary sheet does represent an annual total. Gross monthly sales in 1939 ranged between $10,000 and $35,000, the highest being for Christmas sales. According to these monthly sales sheets, the 1939 gross total was close to the $230,000 of the previous year. Although Rorimer became critically ill in September 1939 and died at the end of November, he was listed as having sold a small quantity of merchandise through December of that year. Apparently Rorimer had taken some orders that were not filled until later.[40]

Monthly profits ranged considerably in 1939—from 5 percent to 30 percent—but typically from 20 percent to 25 percent. Another single sheet from 1938 also lists sales by individual salesmen. On this sheet, however, markups on merchandise sold ranged between 25 percent and 47 percent, and if Rorimer's Statler fee is included, his total markup was 74 percent. After Rorimer's salary and commission are deducted (both are represented by a single figure), his sales profit was 40 percent.[41] Salesmen's commissions were based on the value and amount of merchandise sold, and some notion of this quantity can be gained from the payroll sheets.

Information about the specific merchandise bought and sold by Rorimer-Brooks can be found in an "Inventory Book" from 1940.[42] The most common acquisition dates listed in this book are 1939 and 1940, indicating a constant turnover of merchandise, but other items have dates in the 1920s and one as early as 1911. This would indicate that rather than reduce prices of earlier acquired items, it was not uncommon to keep these older pieces. In fact, prices of these goods were eventually increased in keeping with current inventory pricing. There is a simple explanation for this, given the nature of the business: obsolescence was unusual. Antiques or antique reproductions obviously do not go out of fashion like new designs. On the contrary, antiques would respond more like investments than old inventory and actually increase in value under normal economic circumstances. For example, an "Antique Spanish Walnut Side Chair" circa 1700, purchased in 1917 for ten dollars, was priced at sixty-five dollars in 1940. This 650 percent markup could not have occurred if the item had been recently acquired. Similarly, a "Carved Wood Wall Bracket" purchased in 1911 for fifteen dollars was listed at eighty-five dollars in 1940. Other examples of items purchased from companies and individuals for much less than the later retail price can be found throughout this "Inventory Book."

Not all old inventory, even if antique, had its price raised; some prices had to be reduced to move the item out. For example, a "Small Brass Doorknocker" purchased in 1915 for five dollars was reduced to two dollars in 1940. This was unusual though, since only a small percentage of the inventory remained in the studio for more than a year or two. Price reductions and increases were the exception at Rorimer-Brooks. Because the mainstay of the company was its custom-made furniture, prices were predetermined, and this merchandise was not held long enough to become inventory. Only purchased items were stocked and included in the "Inventory Book," many of which were special orders that sold immediately. (A list of sources from which Rorimer-Brooks purchased merchandise for resale can be found in appendix B.) Rorimer-Brooks was not large enough to warehouse goods or handle any quantity of items that were not expected to sell quickly, so the usual markup was 50 percent.

The categories of merchandise in the book are of interest, because they indicate the types and amount of merchandise purchased by Rorimer-Brooks. The Show Room section, which includes furniture, is the largest, followed by Lamps and Shades, Pictures and Mirrors, Ornaments, and Fabric, Tapestry, and Rugs. This inventory book, like the small "Shop Detail Book," holds valuable information about a company whose other records had been destroyed. Even though 1940 is the only date covered, the book is probably representative of other years as well. Because the "Shop Detail Book" includes only furniture made by Rorimer-Brooks, and the "Inventory Book" contains only items purchased elsewhere, they complement one another and together provide an overview of items carried by the firm. These two documents may also indicate the volume of business transacted during the depression. If it can be assumed that this volume was greater before the 1930s, then the approximate size of Rorimer-Brooks can be imagined. The lists of client names and of companies that supplied merchandise help to place Rorimer-Brooks within a more specific context, and these names may also aid further research.

One other "Inventory Book," dated 1939, contains lists of materials, such as wood, hardware, and fabric samples.[43] Although these lists may have limited use, they complement the other available information for that date. The only other document containing inventory is also dated 1940 and marks the turning point in the company's history and the end of an era. This is the Parke-Bernet sales catalog of the estate of the late Louis Rorimer. The total inventory at the time of Rorimer's death was substantial for a company that occupied only one building. According to Hummel, fabrics alone, including carpets, were valued in excess of $100,000. Ten of the employees, including Herbert Cave, Robert Boone, and Hummel, "bought" the company for one dollar. Rorimer's only son, James, owned the building at 2232 Euclid Avenue and rented it to the new owners of Rorimer-Brooks.[44] Some of the inventory remained with the company but most went to the estate, with the Cleveland Trust Company acting as the executor and trustee. The family selected 586 choice lots to be auctioned in New York. The auction was held in April 1940, just five months after Rorimer died, at the Parke-Bernet Galleries at 30 East Fifty-seventh Street. The 586 lots in the sale included furniture, fabrics, rugs, tapestries, paintings, lamps, modern pottery and glass, and wallpapers.[45] After the sale, unsold items were returned to Cleveland and placed on consignment at Rorimer-Brooks, Inc. (changed from Rorimer-Brooks Studios).

No price estimates were supplied in the catalog, but the *New York Times* later reported that the total amount realized for the three-day sale was a mere $19,900.[46] The average price paid per lot cannot be determined because many of the items did not sell and were returned to Cleveland. The highest price paid for a single lot was $360 for a twenty-two foot by twelve foot Sarouk carpet.

The assortment of items placed up for auction not only indicates what one particular company valued in the 1930s, from antique to modern, it also suggests the range of decorative art that was available and most desirable. Many of the items are evidence of the kinds of objects Rorimer had been bringing back from Europe on his frequent buying trips. In addition to fine eighteenth-century and earlier antiques from Europe, China, and the Middle East, Rorimer was interested in many of the contemporary European decorative artists working in modern styles, such as Art Deco.

One Art Deco artist who interested Rorimer was Jean Mayodon, a leading French ceramist working with decorated faience, a fine-glazed pottery. Other French ceramics imported by Rorimer were made by Longwy, a French faience company established in 1798. Its Art Deco designs were done with brightly colored glazes outlined in a black manganese resist with animal, floral, and geometric motifs. Lalique, of course, was the renowned French glassmaker who had opened his own glassworks in 1909, and Rorimer imported Lalique glass to America (perhaps the first to do so). Edgar Brandt was a French metalwork designer whose handwrought iron work made him one of the leading French Art Deco designers. "Hand-Wrought Iron Fire Screen by Edgar Brandt" is illustrated in the auction catalog. It is identical to a version of the screen made in 1924, which was one of several objects in a traveling exhibition of works from the 1925 Paris Exposition. Rorimer acquired his screen in Paris from Brandt, who was a personal acquaintance.[47]

French artists and companies dominated the Art Deco scene because it was primarily a French style, but other countries in Europe had their own special versions as well. Orrefors, the famous Swedish glassworks, produced modern glass as early as 1916 under the direction of modernist painters Simon Gate and Edward Hald. Rorimer purchased examples of modern Orrefors glass while in Sweden. In ceramics, Sweden's Art Deco style was represented by the Gustavsberg factory under the direction of Wilhelm Kage beginning in 1917. Rorimer is reported to have also been one of the first to import examples of these Gustavsberg ceramics to America.[48]

Items made by Europe's leading modern decorative arts designers and companies represented in the auction catalog of Rorimer's estate confirm his interest in modern design. This interest was not limited to furniture or to his personal design experiments, and it persisted long after his experience at the Paris Exposition in 1925. Rorimer collected many other modern pieces that were not included in the auction. These were produced by other leading modern designers, such as Jean Dunand, the Swiss Art Deco designer working in France with metal and lacquer, and members of the Austrian Wiener Werkstätte, where a variety of materials were used in its distinctly modern styles. Such objects were displayed in Rorimer's "house in the woods" and many remain with his family today. Others have been presented to museums, such as the Cleveland Museum of Art.

The auction catalog is evidence of more than Rorimer's love of modernism, since only a small portion (38 out of 586 items, or 6.5 percent) of the lots are modern. The catalog is filled with antiques from around the world, which illustrate Rorimer's love of beauty and his taste for quality, his connoisseurship. The objects range from Ch'ing Dynasty Chinese porcelains, to seventeenth-century Dutch paintings, to authentic Charles II seventeenth-century English and Louis XV eighteenth-century French furniture, to reproductions of every furniture style considered worthy of reproduction. These attest to Rorimer's appreciation for good design from every era and his ability to transcend the fashion of the moment in order to enhance it with some treasures from the past. But not limited to the past, Rorimer also delighted in the freshness and simplicity of modern pieces, providing that they shared an important feature with his antiques—quality of design and workmanship. That is why the apparent tension between traditional and modern design relaxed in Rorimer's eyes, because beauty was the arbitrator and quality was the common denominator in the decorative arts that he selected.

A high point of the estate auction was part of the extensive collection of hand-blocked wallpapers for which Rorimer-Brooks was noted throughout the profession. Of special interest were those executed by J. Zuber and Company of Rixheim, Alsace, "the best known and oldest firm of manufacturers, who have been in operation since 1797." Also included were examples of some of the few hand-painted lacquered papers existing in America at that time.[49]

Several other nineteenth- and early twentieth-century papers were saved, and these remain with Rorimer's family. For example, a Rococo design by

Desfosse and Karth was illustrated in the auction catalog but was returned to Cleveland after it did not sell.[50] Others from the estate have floral designs, and two extraordinary wallpapers have exotic bird motifs. One with a peacock pattern is a fine example of Art Nouveau, one of the very high style idioms in which Rorimer worked near the turn of the century. The striking green and orange design of parrots and flowers against a black background is probably an early twentieth-century paper, also of unusually fine quality. The color scheme of pastels with black and white is typical of Art Deco, although the wallpaper design is somewhat naturalistic and therefore likely to be of an earlier date.

The company of M. H. Birge and Sons of Buffalo, New York, was an important supplier of wallpapers to Rorimer-Brooks. Birge and Sons began in 1834 as a dry goods store that also carried wallpapers. Its founder, Martin Birge, soon began to stock imported English papers, and in 1846 the store became devoted solely to the sale of wallpapers. In 1875, under the direction of the sons George and Henry Birge, the company turned to manufacturing wallpapers. They became a branch of the National Wallpaper Company in 1895, and five years later were incorporated.[51] During the years that Rorimer dealt with Birge, the company was known for its collection of historic papers. Not only are several lot numbers in the auction catalog examples of Birge papers, but many of the surviving papers still in rolls bear the Birge label. The Birge historic papers were to be used with Colonial Revival antique or antique reproduction furnishings. The care with which Rorimer selected wallpapers is one more instance of his desire to create each interior with a total integrated design and his ability to tap a variety of resources, as well as his use of a wide range of styles.

Besides wallpaper, another important component of any interior is fabric. A good selection of fabrics used by Rorimer-Brooks in the 1920s and 1930s is intact in a single book of fabric samples. Fabrics include cretone, voile, glazed chintz, linen, sateen, satin, antique satin, silk, silk damask, taffeta, brocaded taffeta, progresso cloth, velvets, velveteens, and tapestries. Although prices are not included, one customer's bill indicates that Rorimer charged $8.50 per yard for antique satin in 1936 and $4.50 per yard for chintz in 1937.[52] Colors include every hue in values ranging from soft pastel tints to dark and heavy shades. Patterns and motifs range from solid textures to bold geometric modern designs. None could be considered dreary, and most are as contemporary and appealing today as they were over half a century ago. In fact, many of these fabrics were real state-of-the-art designs for the 1920s and 1930s. One such example was purchased from the American modernist, Paul Frankl. Before Frankl was accepted by the high-style minority of the American public, his "startling designs were considered to be the work of a madman."[53] Even at that early time, presumably prior to 1925, the date marking the beginning of modern decorative art design in America, Rorimer had been one of the first people in America to purchase his fabrics, as Frankl reminded Rorimer at a later meeting.

Rorimer's eye was as keen for future fashion as it was for that of the past. What dictated the imbalanced proportion of historic to avant-garde designs used by his company were the tastes of the moneyed public more than his own. If Rorimer had any regrets, that would have been one—that his audience was not more receptive to radical changes in interior design.

᎒ 4 ᎒

COMMERCIAL WORK

Residential interiors alone did not bring Louis Rorimer notoriety. The commercial accounts, which included major hotels, banks, clubs, and offices, spread the Rorimer-Brooks name to cities across the country.[1] Less known, but also representative of the firm's contribution, were its collaborations with other furniture manufacturers, especially those with mass-production capabilities.

Besides bringing Rorimer national exposure, the commercial clients afforded him the opportunity to create some of the company's most daring designs. Shortly after the 1925 Paris Exposition, modern interior design and furniture was gradually introduced to America, particularly in New York. Rorimer, who regularly commuted to New York from Cleveland, became an intellectual ambassador of the new styles. Rorimer could import exquisite European antiques, custom make quality reproductions, and create radically modern pieces and place them together under one roof successfully, whether in his studios or for a client. An example of this unlikely eclecticism can be seen in Rorimer's prize account, that of the Statler Hotel chain.

The greatest audience of Rorimer's interior design work was the result of his long association with Ellsworth Statler. This began shortly after a committee of Cleveland civil and industrial leaders wrote to Statler in 1910 inviting him to discuss their need of a first-class hotel. Statler came at once. Over lunch with James P. Dempsey, of the law firm of Squire, Sanders and Dempsey, Statler suggested that although Cleveland was still a one-street city, Superior Avenue being the center of its first-class business district, the hotel should be built on "the street of the future." They both agreed that Euclid Avenue would be an appropriate site, specifically a lot at the corner of Euclid and Twelfth Street that was owned by Charles L. Peck, a past president of the Cleveland Chamber of Commerce.[2]

The property, with 104 feet of frontage on Euclid and 379 feet on East Twelfth, had been purchased by Peck for $150,000 in 1900. By 1911, when Statler Hotels Company was about to sign a lease, the property was valued at

$750,000. Peck made the land available at a reasonable $32,500 annually for ninety-nine years "without reappraisal or re-evaluation." One of the largest and finest hotels in America was to have sixteen stories with more than 800 rooms and 800 baths for an estimated cost of $2 million for the building and at least an additional one-half million for the furnishings. Statler was committed to some out-of-town companies, such as International Silver and Syracuse China, but most services and skills were purchased in Cleveland. George B. Post and Son was selected as the architectural firm to design the building, with W. Sydney Wagner as the working architect.[3]

Statler, aware of his inadequacy in the field of interior decoration, solicited opinions in Cleveland to help him decide which decorator to engage. The unanimous choice was Louis Rorimer. Because Statler feared that he could not relate well to an artist, it was fortunate for both men that Rorimer was also an astute businessman. According to Statler's biographer Floyd Miller, "When they met, Statler beheld a man of thirty-eight years with a square, rather fleshy face and a firm chin. Through steel-rimmed glasses he observed the world with both curiosity and equanimity." Statler invited Rorimer to submit a competitive bid for the design of one guestroom. When they met the next month to discuss the bids, Statler waved Rorimer's watercolor rendering in the air and said, "I like what you've got here, but my God, man, you want as much to do one room as a whole floor cost in my Buffalo house." "Yes, I've been in your Buffalo hotel," Rorimer replied quietly, "and it does give that impression."[4] Statler had a sense of humor and Rorimer got the job, which began a business relationship with the Statler Hotels that would outlive Statler, who died in 1928.

Rorimer was given a free hand to make the public rooms as elegant as he saw fit, and each lobby resembled a museum filled with European art treasures. Statler also felt a need to reserve a block of inexpensive rooms for the traveling man. This section was in such demand that one year after the hotel was opened, Statler purchased a plot of adjacent land and constructed a new wing with an additional 300 economical rooms.

A grand opening for the main hotel was held on the night of October 18, 1912, with a charity ball to entertain leading citizens of Cleveland. The formal public opening of the Hotel Statler Cleveland at the northwest corner of Euclid Avenue and East Twelfth Street was held the next day. Two great banquets were held on the mezzanine floor, one given by eastern hotel executives in honor of Statler and the other by Peck for his business associates. The 1,000-room building was modern, complete, and was considered to be one of the finest in America. It hosted business and social organizations and special events in its beautiful Rorimer-Brooks-designed ballroom.

The Cleveland Statler was an immediate success, so in January of 1914 construction of the Detroit Statler Hotel began with the same team that worked in Cleveland—George B. Post and Sons as architects and Louis Rorimer as decorator. Its formal opening was on February 6, 1915.[5] The next city to host a Statler Hotel with Rorimer-Brooks interiors was St. Louis. Henry J. Bohn of

Statler Hotel, Cleveland, 1912. Pompeian Restaurant. Neoclassical columns provide the setting for late Neoclassical-style side chairs with a Greek border motif stenciled on the top rails. The theme of geometric symmetry is carried to the carpet. *Courtesy of the Western Reserve Historical Society, Cleveland.*

Hotel World wrote that: "Statler is the father of hotel standardization in America, and that means in the world. . . . When you see the new St. Louis Statler, you see the Detroit and Cleveland Statlers with the latest touches in Statler architecture, equipment, furnishings, and art."[6] Such standardization was economical, enabling larger volume for purchasing. Inventory control was improved, because items such as silver, dishes, glassware, and furnishings could serve as interchangable parts from one hotel to another. Rorimer even decorated guestrooms in such a way that draperies, spreads, and rugs could be interchanged because of their related color schemes.

In 1917 when the Hotel Pennsylvania was being built in New York, the architects were uneasy about the prospects of having a Midwestern decorator in

Statler Hotel, Cleveland, 1912. Reception rooms, parlor floor with piano and antique furnishings. Queen Anne-style side chairs, Chinese-style armchairs with open fretwork backs, and Chinese porcelains give these areas an atmosphere of casual formality. Because Rorimer filled the Statler lobbies with authentic antiques, these furnishings may be authentic, rather than copies made in his shops. *Courtesy of the Western Reserve Historical Society, Cleveland.*

charge of furnishings. But Statler trusted Rorimer's aesthetic judgment implicitly, and although minor changes were made in color and design, Rorimer's artistic concepts were used throughout the hotel. Even the architects admitted that this Midwestern decorator had more sophistication than they expected.

Costly imported handmade articles were difficult to obtain during the war, and Rorimer made use of American machine-made millwork for the Pennsylvania. Rugs and fabrics were also domestically made, and even the antiques and objets d'art Rorimer had purchased abroad for other Statler Hotels were replaced with specially fabricated ornamental pieces. As in other Statler Ho-

Statler Hotel, Cleveland, 1912. Lattice Room with richly textured walls and ceiling and patterned carpet. Hepplewhite-style side chairs are lined up against the walls as might have been done in the eighteenth century. *Courtesy of the Western Reserve Historical Society, Cleveland.*

tels, Rorimer personally designed most of the furniture in the public rooms. What he did not manufacture in his Cleveland workrooms, he ordered from a leading American firm. As with other Statler Hotels, Rorimer used standardized color schemes to allow for mass purchasing of bedroom furnishings. Light neutral colors such as beiges and grays were used for walls; taupe, blue, or black were used in Axminster carpets; and taupe, blue, and rose were on drapery and upholstery fabric.[7]

Rorimer's relationship with Statler was so successful that he became a director of the company, a major stockholder, and "the only one who could say no to the boss and make it stick." He continued to furnish and redecorate the hotels, including the earliest Buffalo Statler, until he died. When interviewed in 1928 Rorimer had just completed a modern art roof garden for the St. Louis Statler and was on his way to do the same at the Hotel Pennsylvania.[8]

In 1938 Rorimer completed new dining areas consisting of lounge bars and terrace rooms for dining and dancing in both the Cleveland and Detroit Statlers. The 6,840-square-foot Detroit terrace room, which could accommodate at least 300 guests, was one of the largest dining rooms in Detroit. The 770-square-foot dance floor looked like "a brownish island of polished maple set in a bluish-green sea of carpet." Other colors used in the room's scheme were oyster white, ebony black, firecracker red, and gold. The style was called Modern Empire and featured slim pillars on the borders of the room.

The bar of the Detroit Statler was curved and could accommodate more than twenty guests along its 54-foot length. Behind the bar was a thousand-square-foot mirror which reflected both the lounge and Terrace Room. The bar was walnut trimmed in ebony black and gold, and the stools had red morocco leather tops and platinum-tinted aluminum legs reinforced with gold color bands. Rorimer designed the carpet to tie into the color scheme of the room with its walnut woodwork, gold trim, red leather, and green of the adjoining stairs and Terrace Room carpets. The bar was located on the lowest of five levels, with the terrace of the Terrace Room being on the highest.

In Cleveland the well-known Pompeian Room and three stores were removed to make way for the new modern rooms, which included a lounge bar, terrace room, small ballroom, and two conference rooms. Their motif was bacchanalian with bas-relief figures created by Cleveland artists Glen Shaw and Walter Sinz under Rorimer's personal direction.

The lounge bar was modern with easy chairs and large tables designed by Rorimer-Brooks. An elliptical sunken dance floor was considered the most striking feature of the Cleveland terrace room. The color scheme was peacock blue, oyster white, light lacquer red, ebony black, and gold. One entire wall was covered with flesh-tinted mirror.[9] As stated in the *Western Hotel and Restaurant Reporter:* "Louis Rorimer . . . official decorator for the Hotels Statler Company, was in full charge of the rooms in both cities and practically all their furnishings were created in his shops. The splendid artistic success of the new rooms is directly due to his genius, and it is safe to say that these rooms are not equalled anywhere in this country."[10] Rorimer also received praise for the Boston Statler in a letter from William E. Lescaze, modernist architect, AUDAC member, and designer of modern exhibits at Loeser's Department Store in Brooklyn (quoted in chapter 2).

Before Statler married his second wife, Alice, he had purchased the Long Island mansion owned by comedian Ed Wynn. Statler brought Alice and Rorimer to the estate in 1927 to discuss the remodeling and redecoration of the huge eclectic frame structure. Eventually Alice Statler and Rorimer became good friends and corresponded by letter between visits. Alice had tried to persuade Rorimer to move to New York, and in a letter from the Hotel Pennsylvania she wrote: "Elsie DeWolfe is putting her things on sale here—we went in yesterday to have a look and I never saw such a truck in my life. . . . You did make a mistake not coming to New York—when I see what some of these folks here get away with."[11]

One month before Rorimer's sudden and fatal illness Alice was planning to visit Rorimer and his wife Edith at their summer home. Alice wrote to say that a "tragedy" had just occurred. A mirror fell from the wall of her apartment and broke a blue jar. She asked Rorimer if he could get another like it, and then ironically remarked, "Blessed is he who hath nothing!" Twelve years earlier the thought probably would not have occurred to Alice Statler, when her husband gave Rorimer carte blanche to add a new wing and to go to Europe to purchase the best antiques he could find to furnish their new home. Rorimer often went to Europe to shop for Statler, such as in 1926 when he went to Spain and England to furnish and decorate the Boston Statler.[12]

Rorimer's connoisseurship of European antiques added a special dimension to his American interiors that often educated his clients in addition to providing aesthetic pleasure. Statler and others trusted Rorimer to select items of great historic, aesthetic, and monetary value. Rorimer's taste was the result of years of study and exposure. Through his selections, Statler could elevate his own taste while enjoying the status of owning the objects. According to Miller: "Rorimer's association with Statler made him wealthy and famous, but these were secondary to a greater satisfaction. He saw in the hotels a chance to educate and elevate the American cultural level. He made each lobby something of a museum, exposing the traveler, perhaps for the first time, to excellence in art. He was not entirely abandoning his role as teacher."[13]

Rorimer's reputation for excellence spread beyond Cleveland and his role in the Statler chain. Hotels from Boston, Massachusetts, to Portland, Oregon, followed Statler's lead and sought out Rorimer's company to fill their decorating needs. The most prestigious of these to contribute to Rorimer's expanding portfolio was the Greenbrier at White Sulphur Springs, West Virginia. In a 1931 article in *Hotel World Pictorial* the Greenbrier resort was described as follows:

> Take seventy-five hundred acres of wooded mountains, rollicking streams, rolling golf lands, and winding trails, add six hundred spacious guest rooms, a 650-seat dining room and thirty-five six and eight-room cottages dotting the surrounding parkland. Then with these include a mountain stream swimming pool, an airplane landing field, three golf courses, one hundred and twenty-five saddle horses, and a dozen or more sport and vacation features plus a 125-year background of historic and social prestige.[14]

This background began as early as 1778 when White Sulphur Springs in the Allegheny Mountains of West Virginia was first conceived as a resort location. Its first hotel, built in 1808, and its first private cottages in 1816 were the beginning of what would become the largest hotel building in the world, the Grand Central Hotel, completed in 1858. By 1931 the Greenbrier had gone through two major phases of expansion and modernization—the first in 1913 with the completion of the first Greenbrier Hotel, and then between April of 1930 and March of 1931 when the hotel was virtually rebuilt. A 350-room addition was designed by the Cleveland architectural firm of Philip L. Small, Inc., who then contracted Rorimer-Brooks to furnish and decorate the interiors. Rorimer-Brooks decorated not only the new addition, but many of the original 250 rooms as well.[15] When the project was completed, guest capacity was one thousand, dining room capacity was five hundred, and auditorium and convention hall capacity was six hundred.

The guest rooms were spacious, many with large French doors opening on balconies, most with painted or paneled wall surfaces, and carpeted floors. Features considered to be modern included enclosed radiators, heat registers, chromium bathroom fixtures, tub and shower combinations, French telephones, and pneumatic door checks. Rooms of special interest included the "Virginia Room," a penthouse apartment called the "President's Suite," an approach to the main and private dining rooms known as "Paradise Row," and the large addition to the north end called "Old White." The additions to the Greenbrier nearly doubled its guest capacity and included a new auditorium with full concert, lecture, and motion picture capacity, enlarged lobby, lounges, library, outside sun terrace running the length of the building, and what may have been one of America's earliest enclosed shopping malls.

The furnishings throughout the Greenbrier were in Colonial Revival styles. In the lobby were floral upholstered wing chairs, Chippendale-style camel-back sofas, Federal-style upholstered armchairs, and Empire-style tables with reel and twist turned legs. In the main dining room and Terrace Room were hundreds of Duncan Phyfe-style tablet-backed side chairs around both round and square dining tables. The ballroom was also Neoclassical with an elaborate Adam-style plaster ceiling and Federal-style square-backed arm chairs. Other formally furnished public rooms included Chippendale-style chest-on-chests, Federal-style breakfront bookcases and sofas, and Empire-style drum tables. Guest rooms were furnished in informal country styles. Bed posts and chair and table legs were of lathe-turned and painted wood. Other guestroom furniture included upholstered chairs with ottomans, dressers, and desks. Rorimer's style choices for the Greenbrier fall within about a fifty-year span, from the mid-eighteenth century to just after 1800. Although the conveniences were modern, furnishings were all in correct Colonial Revival styles. Rorimer's use of these historic styles at the Greenbrier was not arbitrary. Furnishings were appropriate to the architecture of the structure housing them and to the hotel's history. In 1942 the U.S. Army used the Greenbrier for a hospital and removed most of the interior decor. After World War II the hotel was completely redecorated by Dorothy Draper of New York, and little if any of Rorimer's decor remained.[16]

Another important commission given to Rorimer-Brooks took its name from the Greenbrier Resort, but was located in Cleveland. The Greenbrier Suite on the twelfth floor was part of the office complex of the Van Sweringen brothers, located on the thirty-sixth floor of Cleveland's landmark, the Termi-

74

Greenbrier Hotel, 1930s. View of the Virginia Room with murals depicting the history of White Sulphur Springs, by Cleveland artist William C. Grauer. *Courtesy of the Greenbrier, White Sulphur Springs, West Virginia.*

nal Tower. The Van Sweringens' railroad empire in 1930 included 30,000 miles of track and other equipment worth, at one time, $3 billion. This included the Chesapeake and Ohio Railroad, which had owned the Greenbrier Resort for twenty years.[17] Cleveland was the home base of that empire, and the offices included the Greenbrier Suite. Rorimer-Brooks was in charge of all the Van Sweringens' decorating needs.

The Greenbrier Suite was lined with rich wood paneling, doors, trim, staircases, and other embellishments. Although the suite has since been redecorated, much of its original decor remained until recently, including furniture made by Rorimer-Brooks. A Federal-style dining room with a hand-painted Chinese scenic wall covering is believed to have been original, as were the Duncan

Greenbrier Hotel, 1930s. President's Parlor, upper lobby. The portrait of George Washington is a copy of a Gilbert Stuart in a setting of late Federal-style furnishings. *Courtesy of the Greenbrier, White Sulphur Springs, West Virginia.*

Phyfe lyre-backed chairs, sideboard, and dining table.[18] Other Rorimer-Brooks furniture found throughout the suite included an enormous seventeenth-century-style oak table with giant foliate-carved acorn pedestal supports.

The Charles II/William and Mary caned chair must have been a favorite of Rorimer's because interpretations of it are found in some of his most interesting interiors. Examples of this chair design in the Greenbrier Suite, unlike earlier oak versions with Spanish feet and gilding, are of mahogany and have less typical scroll feet. There is no carving on the back panels, but carved crest rails, front stretchers, and scroll legs were features used on other Rorimer-Brooks chairs in this style. A small William and Mary-style table placed be-

Greenbrier Hotel, 1930s. Garden Room (formerly called the Organ Lobby) directly off the main lobby. The table is set for afternoon tea, which is still served here. Wicker furniture, potted palms, and lace tablecloths provide an air of romantic elegance. *Courtesy of the Greenbrier, White Sulphur Springs, West Virginia.*

tween the pair of chairs coordinated with several similar pieces found throughout the suite and offices.

The Chesapeake and Ohio Railroad (Chessie) retained the Greenbrier Suite (and the Greenbrier Resort) plus other offices in the Terminal for half a century after the Van Sweringen brothers died. These offices were also filled with Rorimer-Brooks pieces, all in historic Anglo-American styles. The conference table and chairs are examples of Rorimer-Brooks's use of artistic license with historic styles. Typical William and Mary cup-and-trumpet turned table legs are connected by serpentine stretchers similar to those on the sideboard and buffet at Bigsbluff, the country summer home of Rorimer's brother. The

Greenbrier Suite, Terminal Tower, Cleveland. Rich wood paneling is found throughout the suite. The William and Mary-style table and pair of Charles II-style cane and mahogany side chairs are representative of the period from which Rorimer adapted many of the pieces found throughout the suite. Although the original chairs would have been of walnut in 1690, Rorimer chose mahogany for his otherwise accurate reproductions in 1930. *Photo by the author, courtesy of the Chesapeake and Ohio Railroad.*

drawer pulls and table skirt cutouts are also correct for the William and Mary style. However, a large conference table was not a William and Mary item (nor was a sideboard), and the style of the armchairs placed around the table is of the Federal period of the next century. The woods and finish of the table and chairs match, but this alone does not account for the compatibility of the unlikely combination of styles from 1700 and 1800. Rorimer's sense of proportion and design enabled him to mix these and other styles successfully.

A large partner's desk is another example of the furniture in the Terminal Tower until Chessie left Cleveland in 1986. Originally there were three desks in the Chessie set, and one is currently being used in the president's West Wing Study of the White House, where it has been since 1974.[19]

Three of the most notable real estate ventures of the Van Sweringens were the Union Terminal; Shaker Heights, the model suburb whose success was directly tied to the rapid transit line from the Union Terminal; and Shaker Square, a model shopping center considered to be one of the most attractive in America. The Square contained twelve Georgian-style buildings designed by Philip L. Small and Charles Bacon Rowley. Beginning with Moreland Courts, numerous fine apartment buildings were built in the area around the Square. Because Rorimer had so much business in Shaker Heights, he opened up a branch studio at Shaker Square next to Shaker Tavern, which he also decorated and furnished. Since the downtown location was preferred by most, and the Shaker Square showroom did not get enough walk-in traffic, the experiment lasted only a few years.[20]

Even the Van Sweringens' private home was done entirely by Rorimer-Brooks. A wonderful country estate fifteen miles east of the Terminal Tower in Hunting Valley was named Daisy Hill. It took seven years to develop at a cost of $2 million and consisted of a main house, stables, nursery, greenhouse, manmade lake, and twenty-two garages. The main house had fifty-four rooms, but the eccentric bachelor brothers shared only one bedroom with twin beds. They used most of the remaining rooms to display their collection of fine antiques, such as Dresden and Spode china and American paintings. One room, called the Dickens Room, held first or limited editions and was special to the two brothers.

Rorimer-Brooks designed and furnished the interior of the Daisy Hill mansion.[21] Although several periods were represented, the theme was early American. All of the furniture was in Colonial Revival styles from the early seventeenth to the early nineteenth centuries. Designs ranged from c. 1600 oak tables with cup-and-cover or column-shaped legs and c. 1700 Welsh-style dressers with legs and stretchers to Duncan Phyfe Regency-style tables. Earlier Neoclassical-style pieces, such as sideboards, were of Sheraton and Hepplewhite designs. Also included were several Queen Anne-style pieces such as high chests of drawers with cabriole legs and slipper feet. Less formal pieces found throughout the Daisy Hill mansion were numerous early eighteenth-century-style banister-backed chairs and a variety of upholstered chairs and sofas.

Although like the Van Sweringens most of Rorimer's clients preferred traditional styles, Rorimer was grateful for the opportunity to specialize in custom-designed and executed furniture and fine one-of-a-kind accessories. Rorimer disapproved of mass-producing furniture, believing that "machines have killed our artistic craftsmen," and there were no facilities for mass production at his studios. When his designs were intended for mass production, it was the exception and little known by his residential clientele. Several instances of collaboration with other companies to mass produce his designs occured. Although no evidence has been found regarding his arrangement with the Aluminum Company of America (now Alcoa), in 1931 it was reported by art editor Robert Bordner in the *Cleveland Press* that Rorimer was "quietly designing" ultramodern metal furniture for them. Other modern aluminum furniture was designed at Rorimer-Brooks by William Green and Andrew Probala. Green designed Art Deco aluminum tables and Probala designed the accompanying side chairs. Aluminum had been used little, if at all, for chairs until this time because the technology for welding the parts together had not been satisfactory. At significant expense, the furniture was executed by General Fireproofing in Youngstown, Ohio, and installed at the Higbee Company Silver Grille

Daisy Hill mansion, Hunting Valley, Ohio, residence of the Van Sweringen brothers. Rorimer served both commercial and residential decorating needs of the brothers and their railroad empire. This bedroom in late Neoclassical Duncan Phyfe-style with canopied four-poster beds is more formal than most of the other rooms. *Photo by Clifford Norton, 1927. Courtesy of the Western Reserve Historical Society, Cleveland.*

Restaurant in downtown Cleveland, where it had been in use from 1931 until December 30, 1989, when the Grille closed and Cleveland lost one of its few remaining Art Deco interiors. A third company that was known to have executed Rorimer-Brooks designs was Dunbar in Indiana, but all that has been found is a small brass plaque that would have been attached to a piece of furniture that reads, "Designed by Rorimer-Brooks Studios, Cleveland, Executed by Dunbar Furniture Manufacturing Company."[22]

While Rorimer-Brooks was in the midst of designing the interior of the Shaker Tavern at Shaker Square, Ray Irvin, who was handling the account, found a photograph of an eighteenth-century chair. Irvin decided to use the chair for the tavern, so he gave the photograph to Andrew Probala. When Probala made the scale drawings, he added double stretchers below the seat for

Daisy Hill mansion, dining area. The custom-made carpet (probably by Rorimer, who also designed carpets), beamed ceiling, and brick fireplace provide a Colonial atmosphere and setting for rush-seat side chairs and seventeenth-century-style turnings on the dining table. *Photo by Clifford Norton, 1927. Courtesy of the Western Reserve Historical Society, Cleveland.*

extra support and because it was customary for men to place their hats under the chair while dining. Since so many were needed, Probala's model was sent to Dunbar to be mass-produced.[23]

At present, the most reliable documented evidence of a relationship between Rorimer-Brooks and another company concerns Taylor Chair of Bedford, Ohio. Fortunately Taylor Chair keeps old records and takes pride in its history. It is "the oldest continuously operating company in the Western Reserve and is thought to be the oldest furniture manufacturer in the nation."[24]

Bedford Township was in the center of the Western Reserve, or "New Connecticut," where the wandering Benjamin Franklin Fitch settled. Fitch was a

Living room of Daisy Hill mansion with extensive use of wood—wide plank flooring, paneling, ceiling beams, and seventeenth-century-style tables—carried through the rich Colonial atmosphere. Contrasting contemporary upholstered pieces and Oriental carpets provide softness and comfort to an otherwise heavily masculine room. *Photo by Clifford Norton, 1927. Courtesy of the Western Reserve Historical Society, Cleveland.*

skilled woodsman and hunter and also made "slat-backed" and "splint-bottomed" chairs for his cabin. They looked just like the ones he had known back in New England, and soon others wanted these well-made chairs in which the drying of the wood was so controlled that neither screws nor glue were necessary to hold them together. The demand for "Fitch Splint Bottom Chairs" soon required an additional cabin, more workers, and new tools. Fitch developed the strap-lathe, which allowed continuous turning, contributed to increased production, and later became a standard machine for the furniture industry. From 1816 to 1844 Fitch produced armchairs, side chairs, rockers,

Art Deco aluminum tables (with plastic laminate tops added at a much later date) and chairs designed for the Silver Grille restaurant of the Higbee Company, Cleveland, in 1931. *Photo by Ramón Piña. Courtesy of the Higbee Company.*

children's rockers, and high chairs. Each one was compact, well-proportioned, and of handcrafted individuality.[25]

William Orville Taylor, one of Fitch's employees, married Fitch's daughter Harriet Martha in 1841. He was born in 1814 and came to the Western Reserve with his family in 1831. Taylor and his father-in-law were progressive businessmen and used every labor-saving and quality-enhancing device known in order to serve the community.[26]

By the mid-1840s Taylor had taken over active management of the company, and late in the decade the company became known as the W. O. Taylor factory. In 1850 Taylor moved the factory to its present location in Bedford, adjoining Tinker's Creek, after a fire destroyed the original building. With water for steam power and the new Cleveland-Pittsburgh Railroad to transport materials in and finished chairs out, the site proved to be an excellent choice. The company grew, and in 1885 it became Taylor Chair Company, a corporation with an issue of one thousand shares of stock. The 1885 catalogs illustrated forty-eight types of chairs, which were mostly rockers, but also included eight varieties of office chairs, one of which revolved and tilted.

Despite the changes, Taylor Chair was consistent in its belief in quality of product, durability, and comfort. By 1904, ninety-one designs were being produced, including nineteen swivel office chairs and its line of ever-popular rockers. A professional designer was mentioned as having been associated with Taylor as early as the mid-1880s; this was Rorimer's friend and former teacher, Herman Matzen. In 1889 one of Matzen's chair designs became Taylor Chair's first patent.[27]

In the 1920s there was "a trend to more individual period offices in the 18th Century, Louis XVI, Tudor, Flemish and Italian Renaissance Styles." So Taylor Chair produced authentic period chair designs as well. The demand for matched suites in period styles increased, and these soon became status symbols. This demand encouraged the alliance between Taylor and a desk factory, Horrocks Desk Company of Herkimer, New York. They coordinated styling, jointly produced catalogs, and sold Horrocks Taylor Executive Suites to a select group of prestige office furniture dealers. It was at this time that Rorimer-Brooks was most involved with the company, which is presently in its seventh generation.[28]

The strongest evidence of the association between these two companies consists of watercolor renderings and pencil drawings by William Green.[29] A sufficient number of these drawings were signed by Green to confirm his execution of the others, which were done in exactly the same style. Similarly, a sufficient number were labeled Taylor Chair or were in the possession of Taylor Chair, indicating that the others were also part of that group. The chairs are representative of the type of office chair designed and produced by Rorimer-Brooks and Taylor Chair in 1930.

In addition to manufacturing chairs, office desks were featured by Taylor Chair after their collaboration with Horrocks Desk. An unusual custom-made American Art Deco desk is an example of the very modern Taylor-Horrocks items offered in 1930. The original drawing for this desk, undoubtedly done by Green, is labeled "The Taylor Chair Co." Other examples of desks, although in more traditional styles, are represented by the drawings.

Other traditionally styled office furniture is pictured and described in Taylor-Horrocks' illustrated catalogs. One example, entitled "Executive Suites" in catalog no. 122, featured several modern pieces including desks, chairs, bookcases, tables, and even smaller matching accessory pieces such as coatracks and wastebaskets. The modern line, called "The Future," was described in the same catalog:

> For the executive who is planning an office in the Trend of Today, whose office design must reflect his own aggressive personality and leadership in the business world, Taylor Chair offers this modern group. Designed by one of America's fore-

most contemporaries, the Future has Vigor and Smartness . . . conservatively streamlined in keeping with the tempo of modern interior architecture. The interior of the desk is engineered for efficiency and convenience, to eliminate loss of time and wasted motion. The fine woods and excellent craftsmanship guarantee it for lifetime service.[30]

These pieces exemplified American Art Deco design inspired by French Art Moderne. Features included veneers matched with extreme precision and absence of raised moldings or other conventional trim that might "mar the smooth flowing lines." Rounded corners (claimed to be an exclusive Taylor feature) and V-matched striped walnut drawer fronts were favored. Rare amboina burl, black lacquer trim, chromium drawer pulls, bleached walnut finish, and chair leather with welts of contrasting colors were among the materials used. All were designed for comfort, utility, and beauty. These features, which were used to describe Taylor-Horrocks desks and other furniture, were also characteristic of some of the finest Art Deco pieces of Europe and America, particularly with regard to the use of rare exotic woods for beautifully patterned veneers and of novel materials such as chromium and lacquer. What made them characteristically American in design was their pronounced rectilinearity. The American skyscraper, a trademark of Paul Frankl, had become the stylistic model for furniture as well as for architecture, although Rorimer felt that the skyscraper was too big and artistically unsuccessful. Simple geometric forms based on the rectangle persisted after the exoticism of Art Deco had faded.[31] Other Green designs for this ultramodern furniture were produced by Taylor but not featured in the catalog.

If the more exotic elements of the Taylor-Horrocks pieces—geometric patterns created by the meticulous placement of matching veneers, the stylized carved feet, and flat stylized columns in place of corners—are eliminated, what remains is the style called Depression Modern that was popular in America in the 1930s. Retaining the essential flavor of Art Deco, Depression Modern pieces were often mass-produced and sold cheaply.[32] Others, while extremely simple and sparse in design, were well made and fashionable, such as furniture made by Rorimer-Brooks for a Shaker Heights residence. Although in poor condition when photographed half a century later, these bedroom storage pieces consisting of drawers and shelf space were originally made with carefully matched veneers. Such pieces were considered very stylish and modern in their day.[33]

In addition to fine veneered pieces in which the grain of the woods created a surface texture and design, there were similarly shaped modern pieces lacquered in solid colors. A desk and bookcase designed and made for Homer H. Johnson was originally green with silver leaf, which has since been painted black. The dentil-pattern border design used by Rorimer in this and other pieces can also be seen in furniture by AUDAC designers such as Frankl.[34] The form of these pieces was also in the manner of Frankl's "skyscraper" designs, which were novel in form rather than in ornamentation. Frankl believed that the furniture in a modern metropolitan apartment should be consistent with the exterior architecture. He designed desks, bookcases, and desk-bookcases in vivid hues, often with the addition of gold or silver leaf.[35] Rorimer's green and silver desk-bookcase was possibly influenced by Frankl's, which were among the most revolutionary designs in America in 1930. But where Frankl enjoyed the advantage of New York's sophisticated market, Rorimer's most modern designs were usually used by his own family and such friends as Johnson. Even the Taylor-Horrocks Art Deco and other modern office furniture was not produced on a large scale. Due to their fine workmanship and subsequent high cost, a clientele with the means to furnish offices in such pieces would have been limited. Because of the extreme design of the furniture, an even rarer audience would have appreciated them.

Rorimer acquired many of his ideas and objects from New York and from abroad, thus contributing to Cleveland becoming part of a broader design network. Since Rorimer did not wish to unsettle his conservative residential clientele, his excursions into modern idioms were sometimes under the guise of collaboration with other companies. Thus he was able to contribute to the modernization of commercial interiors without jeopardizing the confidence of an established residential audience. Companies such as Taylor Chair served as "ghost writers" enabling Rorimer to experiment more creatively than might have been possible otherwise.

American furniture manufacturers were reluctant to participate in the introduction of Art Moderne styles, and decorators were not eager to promote them. Henry-Russell Hitchcock, Jr., observed that by 1928 "products presented at the Paris Exposition in such large and varied numbers and already once incidentally and unsuccessfully introduced into this country by the Wiener Werkstätte, began to appear here through commercial channels rather than through architects and decorators. Indeed it was chiefly in connection with fashion, and by dealers in fashion, that modern furnishing features began to appear in America along with the clothes, accessories, and perfumes of the Paris dressmaker."[36]

It was the department store that eventually contributed the most in acquainting the American public with modern design. The first large modern decorative art exhibition in America was sponsored by Macy's in 1927. The exhibits were international. Later, other large urban department stores began to carry modern furniture and accessories by European and American designers. In 1928 Lord and Taylor exhibited modern interiors by France's top designers.[37]

In addition to department stores, a few avant-garde galleries began to specialize in modern design. In 1928 the Park Avenue Galleries in New York claimed that ninety percent of their decorating jobs were done in the modern manner, whether French or American.[38] Although this was a relatively small establishment, it confirms that New York had the major market for this style. In a 1928 issue of *Good Furniture Magazine*, Nellie Sanford wrote, "With the possible exception of Paris, it is doubtful if another city than New York would offer sufficient field for such individual specialized furniture making in a mode with which only the sophisticates are familiar as a part of daily life."[39]

Rorimer had clients in New York, and he designed and made modern pieces, such as a dining table for his children's apartment.[40] Rorimer-Brooks was commissioned to design modern furnishings for the Chrysler Suite in the new Chrysler Building in New York. Designed by William Van Alen, it was begun on October 15, 1928, and opened to the public on April 1, 1930. It is a prime example of American modernism with outstanding architectural features such as a six-tiered dome finished in polished metal sheets—the first time that sheet steel was used extensively as an exterior finish on an important American building. The office partitions inside were also of steel and made into interchangeable sections enabling floor plans of any office suite to be changed quickly and conveniently. This feature of interchangeability was familiar to Rorimer, who had used it in the Statler Hotels. Both the exterior and interior motifs of the Chrysler Building epitomize American Art Deco. The original drawings for the interior of the Chrysler Suite were done by Andrew Probala while Rorimer was in Europe for one month. When Rorimer returned, he was pleasantly surprised to see that Probala had not just designed simple, contemporary furniture with an Oriental flavor for the suite's rooms, he had drawn alternatives for each piece of furniture as well. After studying Probala's designs, Rorimer initialed his choices, had the furniture made in his shops, and sent everything to New York to be installed.[41]

One of the last interiors Rorimer completed was also in New York, a small but special project in 1938 for his son, James. As a youngster, James had traveled extensively throughout Europe with his family, where Rorimer would "train the children's eyes to see what most tourists would miss." But Rorimer would only take the children to art museums for one hour at a time, because he wanted them to absorb what they saw and then look forward to their return.[42]

James, who at one time planned to please his father by joining Rorimer-Brooks, graduated from Harvard in 1927, and then, at the age of twenty-two, became an assistant in the Decorative Arts Department of the Metropolitan Museum of Art. In 1926 the collection of medieval art that had been presented to the Metropolitan by John D. Rockefeller, Jr., in the previous year was arranged in a branch of the museum called the Cloisters. In 1929 the idea of building a separate structure, to be called the Cloisters, was suggested to James while both the director and the assistant director were away. In 1930 Rockefeller presented land to the city and reserved a portion for what was to be the new Cloisters museum.[43]

The firm of Allen, Collens and Willis, of Boston, designed the building, and Collens worked closely with James Rorimer during the construction, which began in 1934. The younger Rorimer had become the curator of the Department of Mediaeval Art on January 1, 1934, and then of the Cloisters on January 1, 1938. Louis Rorimer, who took a great interest in the evolution of the Cloisters, visited the building site often and offered helpful suggestions. He also made furniture to his son's specifications and donated it for the

The Cloisters, Metropolitan Museum of Art, New York. Rorimer designed, manufactured, and donated the furnishings for the curator's office of the Cloisters in 1938. His son James later became director of the museum. *Courtesy of Mrs. James J. Rorimer.*

curator's office in the tower. In 1938 at the formal dedication, Rorimer said that in some ways it was a pity that his son had already achieved so much at the young age of thirty-three, "since nothing else in his life could ever match the satisfaction of being given the materials to create a masterpiece."[44] But James would have many more creative opportunities during his directorship of the Metropolitan Museum of Art.

❧ 5 ❧

RESIDENTIAL

Large commercial accounts indicate the size and scope of the company, but for elements of style, individual furnishings are the most revealing, especially custom-designed residential work. Ironically these pieces were not often revealed. As one writer observed, "Rorimer-Brooks Studios, nationally known, had some of its finest interiors in its own home town—interiors whose owners treasure their exclusiveness so highly that the public may not see them even in photographs."[1] Clearly, however, Clevelanders of the 1920s evinced a remarkable preference for English styles. The city's elite residential district, Shaker Heights (begun in 1916), self-consciously used English classical (especially Georgian) and picturesque (notably Tudor) and subsequent Colonial Revival architectural styles. Other builders and developers emulating them spread the fashion across the city. Rorimer accommodated homeowners' needs by coordinating interior furnishings with the exterior architecture. Because Shaker Heights was his most significant suburban market, Rorimer furnished these homes in compatible English styles.

The Victorian mansions built along Euclid Avenue's "Millionaires' Row" in the 1880s and 1890s were no longer considered elegant and smart. They were summarily dismissed as sentimental and naive revivals in contrast to what was deemed the thoughtful, academic historicism of the 1920s. Americans wanted a different sort of accuracy in the design of their buildings and furnishings. Those architects and designers who had been trained in Europe and were thought to have a better understanding of the correct use of early styles were suddenly in demand.[2] In 1929 Rorimer was praised because he had "led us out of the stuffy Victorian into a cleaner, clearer, more livable environment."[3]

Although design was Rorimer's primary interest, and he enjoyed combining historic design elements from many European countries in his furnishings, American Colonial Revival styles proved to be the backbone of his business. Most clients wanted interiors that idealized and romanticized premodern America. Homes and furnishings became the vehicle for a popular nostalgia

89

for the past that was equated with a more innocent time, a longing that either ignored or glorified a great deal of pain and sadness.[4]

Rorimer-Brooks featured the styles in the early twentieth century because they were in vogue and because Rorimer was one of the European-trained Americans who could use and promote the styles successfully. Upper-middle-class Americans, especially midwesterners, were increasing in number. Rorimer's clients were part of this group that may have contributed to the persistence of the Colonial Revival styles in architecture and interior furnishings to the present day.

A second and somewhat related set of romantic impulses sprang from the Arts and Crafts movement. For the middle classes the Arts and Crafts, like the Colonial Revival styles, celebrated Anglo-American nativism and rejected the ills of industrialism. Rorimer worked in the Arts and Crafts idiom because he shared its ideals of good design and craftsmanship and he demonstrated distrust in the use of machinery.[5] Straightforwardness of design and construction, clean straight lines, and natural wood finishes characterized Arts and Crafts furniture, particularly in America. English versions had been produced for several decades before the movement crossed the Atlantic, and they were more varied. Embellishments such as carving and medieval (Gothic) references were commonly used in English styling. Rorimer used both.

Because Rorimer-Brooks rarely had its designs mass-produced, many pieces were one-of-a-kind. There are several important consequences for modern researchers. First, the chance of finding many unique pieces after years of relocation is slim. Except for a few known households with their original furnishings, the designs that have most often been located are those made in the greatest numbers. As the handwritten "Shop Detail Book" indicated, once a model number was given to a new design, it was common practice to reuse it for another client. There are therefore more chances that these multiple-use designs will be found, and it is less likely that one-of-a-kind examples of greater aesthetic and historic value will surface. Second, even when a unique piece is discovered, it may not be identified, because there may be nothing to compare it to. Because only some Rorimer-Brooks furniture was labeled, identification must be based only on comparison with documented pieces. Third, because Rorimer did not personally design prototypes destined for mass production as did other modern furniture designers, and because his other responsibilities usually kept him away from the drafting table, examples of his designs are rare. If relatively few pieces were actually designed by Rorimer, then it must be assumed that even fewer exist today. The point is that no Rorimer-Brooks designs for residential furniture were produced in quantity. A limited number of each was made—sometimes only one—so every piece of furniture represents a part of the company's range of style.

One of the first homes furnished entirely with Rorimer-Brooks furniture was Bigsbluff, the summer home of Maurice Rohrheimer, Louis's older brother. Maurice was known as "Big" because of his height and he was fondly called Uncle Big by family members. He discovered the site while hunting some years

90

earlier and built the summer house on a favorite bluff—hence "Bigsbluff." The frame and stone house, designed by Dercum and Beer and completed in 1912, was sited to take advantage of the 150 acres of hills, woods, streams, and farmland in a fashion characteristic of the "organic" designs of contemporary leading modern American architects such as Frank Lloyd Wright.

Each window looks out upon either a natural or cultivated garden. The interior design is comparable to the work of modern German, Austrian, and British architects working between 1910 and 1925.[6] Abundant use of wood integrates the interior and creates a textural effect. The ceiling of the spacious living room is beamed, many of the walls are half-timbered with light pickled pine, floors are hardwood, and floor-to-ceiling cabinets (carved by Rorimer) are built into a dining room wall.

Rorimer's furniture designs at Bigsbluff ranged from the seventeenth to the twentieth centuries. Among the seventeenth-century inspired pieces were ornately carved cane-backed chairs and press cupboards. For the latter Rorimer conveyed age by craftsmanship, materials, and styling. This type of furniture also had unmistakable social significance. Cupboards were important pieces of storage furniture in England and in America, and the most imposing ones were press cupboards and court cupboards, which had a similar appearance and functioned for storage and to display textiles or plate. Although many more English than American seventeenth-century press cupboards survived, many people considered the form American and used them as status symbols on which to display other status symbols. Although functional in both the seventeenth and twentieth centuries, they were neither necessary nor especially practical. They served as emblems of social identification and recognition rather than of physical comfort, unlike, for example, a cane chair, even an ornately carved one.[7]

To taste-conscious twentieth-century American upper-middle-class homeowners who turned to professional architects, decorators, and writers for guidance, the cupboard was stylish. Unlike the limited supply of antiques, reproduction furniture, which could be made to look like anything conceivable from any time or any place, was readily available. Clearly Rorimer promoted historic styles, and there was a reliable market for them, but he did not create the demand so much as he satisfied it. Rorimer optimized his talents and served the public by supplying period antiques, correct reproductions, and fanciful interpretations.

Since most historic styles were known in the early twentieth century, the choices made by members of that society can be revealing. Rorimer's clients trusted him to make choices suitable to their needs and in accordance with current fashion. From a sampling of books on interior design, decoration, and furnishing published between 1903 and 1936, contemporary attitudes regarding the use of period antique, reproduction, and modern furniture can be discerned.[8] Although some authors and decorators advocated the use of only historic styles while others rejected all but the most modern, the majority were somewhere between these extremes, and modern came to be treated as just

Carved oak press cupboard, 1912. (H. 52″, W. 49″, D. 16-1/2″.) *Photo by author, private collection.*

another period style.[9] The issue was not whether antique or modern styles were best suited to the needs of a growing technological society—there was a place for both.

Candace Wheeler, writing at the turn of the century on interior decoration, noted, "There are many reasons why one should be in sympathy with what is called the 'colonial craze'; not only because colonial days are a part of our history, but because colonial furniture and decoration were derived directly from the best period of English art." Though Wheeler recognized the generally high quality of the manufacturing techniques and standards of historic

Anglo-American furniture, she did not necessarily promote the styles. Her advice was to seek out quality regardless of its source. She wrote, "Of course we cannot all have colonial furniture, and indeed it would not be according to the spirit of our time, for the arts of our own day are to be encouraged and fostered." Yet, "the quest of antiques will go on until we become convinced of the art-value and the equal merit of the new."[10]

In 1923 Reginald Townsend, editor of *Country Life* magazine, edited a book comprised of a series of articles selected from the magazine. *The Book of Building and Interior Decoration*, filled with American country houses and interiors, contained "the most authoritative material available" and displayed the "most recent developments in domestic architecture."[11] In a group of the articles entitled "Adapt Your Furniture to Your House," seventeenth- and eighteenth-century Anglo-American styles were featured, with a preference for the early eighteenth century, considered to be the most refined and most outstanding period for design and craftsmanship. Another article posed the question of whether antique or antique reproduction furniture was the most desirable. Modern or otherwise original designs were not even considered. The recommendations offered in a book containing "the most recent developments" were to mix periods, namely the seventeenth and eighteenth centuries, and to mix national styles, namely Italian, French, and Anglo-American, in the same room.

Another 1923 publication, *The Principles of Interior Decoration* by Bernard Jakway, noted that period decoration was a twentieth-century phenomenon. Not only furniture, but entire rooms of woodwork, fireplaces, and other interior architecture, especially from Europe, were ripped out of their original contexts and installed in American homes. A negative attitude toward modern design seemed to contribute to the prevailing positive attitude toward historicism. "The decorator finds himself the heir of all the ages," Jakway observed. "It is clear that we must use historic furniture until our own designers can give us something better; if, indeed the thing be ever possible." There was little doubt in Jakway's mind that historic styles were the best currently available. The question was of antique versus antique reproduction, and this time the choice was viewed in terms of simple economics: those who could afford to import European antiques did so, and those who could not, purchased reproductions.[12]

But Jakway was describing the state of the art rather than his personal philosophy of interior design. In fact, he believed that the use of period or period-style furnishings should probably be curtailed. "[I]t is now considered by many decorators . . . to be the smart thing to furnish a dining room with a refectory table and benches. Thus we find otherwise sensible people sitting on long, narrow and uncomfortable benches, and crowded at either side of a very narrow table which, as used historically, had diners on one side only—the side very near a wall, which offered protection against a surprise attack or a sudden knife-thrust from behind"[13]

Jakway, like Rorimer, was neither for nor against period design, because beauty can be found in various times and places. The issue was whether the designs were appropriate to modern needs. "It is in fact only in the degree that an historic style can be so modified in practice as to adapt it to the requirements of comfortable modern life that it is properly of interest to the decorator of today."[14] This statement sums up the attitude shared by thoughtful decorators and designers of the early 1920s, including Rorimer. In fact, such an attitude set the stage for the radical modification of historic style, especially neoclassicism, that began to occur in America after exposure to the Art Moderne styles at the 1925 Paris Exposition. Yet change was resisted by all but the most daring designers and writers about design for some time.

For example, in a book entitled *The Practical Book of Learning Decoration and Furniture,* published in 1926, the author advises the reader to "REMEMBER: That in all the world for a hundred years there has been no great designer of furniture. That about 1840 all the decorative arts failed. That during what is called the 'Victorian-General Grant Period' all countries lost not only the ability to design but even the sense of good taste as well."[15]

In addition to this attitude, which was undoubtedly taught in schools, the only countries recognized as having made contributions were Italy, France, Spain, and England, and the only styles worth considering were Renaissance, Baroque, Rococo, and Neoclassical.[16] It is no wonder that Rorimer's clientele were reluctant to try his modern designs throughout most of his career.

Modern furniture became recognized in America a decade later, as indicated in publications such as the small but informative guide by Lurelle Guild, *Designed for Living: The Blue Book of Interior Decoration* in 1936. Among the choices for styles of furniture and decorations, the author outlined eight distinct periods, beginning with Elizabethan. Rather than considering neoclassicism the final period (the Victorian period is simply ignored), a new period is suggested, and it is called Modern.[17]

Modern furniture is characterized by Guild as having functional simplicity, minimal use of detail, exotic woods in which the grain supplies the surface design, such as amboina, rosewood, tigerwood, thuya, hollywood, bleached mahogany, and blond maple. Rorimer had also favored exotic and bleached woods, but much earlier, and he used them in interiors and furnishings such as at Bigsbluff in 1912. Other modern materials listed by Guild included various plastics (such as bakelite), glass, crystal, plastic laminate, aluminum, chromium, and mirrored surfaces. Yet even at the relatively late date of 1936, Guild advocated a blend of period styles. Modern items were confined primarily to the largest cities, and then most often were used only in the bedrooms.[18]

Any discussion of colonial antique and antique reproduction furniture in America in the 1920s and 1930s must include some mention of Wallace Nutting, collector, author, and dealer in American antiques and their reproductions. His writing was not necessarily scholarly, and he was not a purist in making his reproductions. In fact, he was at least as much an entrepreneur as a connoisseur. His philosophy, very simply put, was "copy and avoid bad taste" because, he believed, "The limit of styles has been fixed at the end of the Empire period, which indeed brings us to the beginning of the degraded styles."[19]

94

This opinion has a familiar ring to it, probably because it was expounded by other writers at this time, such as Edward Stratton Holloway.

One of Nutting's most notable achievements was the compilation of 5,000 photographs of American furniture, primarily from the seventeenth and eighteenth centuries, in three volumes entitled *Furniture Treasury* in 1928. He was perhaps the most ambitious and thorough collector and disseminator of colonial styles of his time, the same time that Rorimer imported originals and reproduced copies of similar pieces. Nutting's enthusiasm for these styles certainly influenced a broad audience through personal contact and his publications. Because many of Rorimer's colonial pieces predate 1912, it is unlikely that he was influenced by Nutting. Besides, most of Rorimer's antiques were purchased in Europe, and he used them as models for reproductions.[20]

Rorimer was comfortable enough with history to be able to play with it, and his material expressions were not just tables and chairs. They were works of art by a man with a love of beauty and history, with an uncanny sense of design, with a respect for materials, and with the wit to put them all together successfully. When furnishing Bigsbluff he mixed styles throughout the house, within each room, and on single pieces. Wild, yet entirely agreeable, eclecticism characterized some of Rorimer's best work. A bedroom set with Empire characteristics is done with veneers in circassian walnut, a rare and costly wood. Although similar to Biedermeier in form, Rorimer's decision to use richly grained exotic woods as surface treatment anticipated French Art Moderne techniques. Other pieces with Neoclassical influences include an armchair with dolphins carved on the back splat and pendant, bellflower, and acanthus leaf inlays on all smooth surfaces and a tub-shaped chair. But the shape of the latter and its unusual feet have elements of contemporary French Art Nouveau furniture, as Rorimer well knew from his regular trips to Europe.[21] He put similarly carved feet on a boxy low-backed seventeenth-century-style chair with an upholstered Moorish arch on its back.

Rorimer employed arches and other Gothic elements for a hexagonal lamp table with storage compartments. The ogee arches joining each pair of legs, carved quatrefoils, and applied shields are derived from Gothic design. Yet their recombination in this table reflects the tenets of English Arts and Crafts motifs.

Other Rorimer furniture expressed the Arts and Crafts idiom in a very modern and exceptional fashion. An enormous thirteen-foot trestle dining table with a dark finish and adjustable drop leaves and extensions is an adaptation that is both simple and functional. Another imaginative Arts and Crafts piece is a light oak narrow side table with Gothic quatrefoil cutouts at each end. Next to it stands a curious trestle table of bleached oak with distinctly Jacobean vasiform turnings. Its spare design and its placement next to other light oak Arts and Crafts pieces suggests an Arts and Crafts label. While the table's style is not at all typical of Arts and Crafts, its meaning is. This eclecticism exemplifies the subtlety with which Rorimer made artistic statements.

Another example of furniture with which Rorimer seems to have condensed time is the dining room set at Bigsbluff.[22] Although the set has historic

Detail of carved dolphin on back splat of Neoclassical-style armchair of inlaid and painted wood and upholstered seat, 1912. *Photo by Erik Liu, private collection.*

elements, such as late seventeenth-century legs and stretchers, they are combined with motifs from a much later date. The diagonal geometric pattern of matched veneers presages American Art Deco of 1930 more than it harkens back to Federal-style veneers and inlays, and the stylized carved birds and flowers on the sideboard, buffet, and dining table, although inspired by naturalistic Renaissance motifs, likewise forecast Art Deco. Foliate carving on dining table pedestal supports add a British Arts and Crafts flavor to an already eclectic ensemble. The set embodies Rorimer's ideas in about 1912.

The most outstanding piece at Bigsbluff and one of Rorimer's most significant early pieces is an oak and oak-veneer plant stand. This graceful table hints at Art Nouveau in the curve of its feet, while the stylized carved rose, stained to mimic bronze patina, is indicative of that blend of Art Nouveau and

Oak tub-shaped chair with unusual carved feet, 1912. (H. 31-1/4'', W. 25-1/4'', D. 23-1/2''.) *Photo by the author, private collection.*

Carved oak and upholstered armchair with Moorish arch and same feet as tub chair, 1912. (H. 36-3/4″, W. 23″, D. 23″.) *Photo by Erik Liu, private collection.*

Hexagonal table c. 1906. (H. 30'', W. 28''.) Carved oak Charles II-style side chair with caned back and seat. (H. 52'', W. 17-1/2'', D. 16-1/2''.) Rorimer's ability to mix styles from different centuries in one room and even on one piece can be seen in this turn-of-the-century Arts and Crafts table with two seventeenth-century-style chairs made about 1912. *Photo by Patrick Kunklier, private collection.*

Arts and Crafts known as the Glasgow School. Although it is not known whether Rorimer was in Scotland, his frequent travels to England and Germany and general interest in all modern European design would suggest that he was exposed to the work of, if not acquainted with, Glasgow School designers. Since Arts and Crafts was more an attitude and a philosophy than a style, and since Art Nouveau was more of a decorative style than a philosophy, the two could complement each other in a single design and could produce an object that was more aesthetically pleasing and philosophically satisfying than if a designer adhered to a single mode. These hybrids were neither English nor French, because neither culture would openly admit to having borrowed from the other. Objects that demonstrate an emphasis on extreme verticality and use stylized roses as a motif were made by architect-designer Charles Rennie Mackintosh and other Glasgow School designers in materials such as metal, wood, ceramics, and textiles. Furniture with straight legs or with smooth legs and inward-curving feet were designed by Eugene Gaillard of France, Henri van de Velde of Belgium (an acquaintance of Rorimer), and Mackintosh, all of

99

Oak and oak-veneer Glasgow School-style plant table, 1912 (or earlier). (H. 36″, W. 15″, D. 11-3/4″.) *Photo by Erik Liu, private collection.*

whose work had been exhibited in Europe since the turn of the century, and which Rorimer had undoubtedly viewed.[23]

Another of Rorimer's Arts and Crafts interpretations is an oak dining set—oval extension table on a pedestal, sideboard, buffet, and eight matching chairs—now in a private collection in Maine. The set is labeled "Hand Made at the Rohrheimer-Brooks Studios . . . Cleveland" paradoxically using a pre-1906 spelling of Rorimer's name in conjunction with a partner he acquired in 1910. However, the label and the style of the furniture would indicate the date of manufacture to be in or about 1910. Stylized carved accents on the cabinet doors, chair backs, and pedestal base are European traits. Mackintosh and E. A. Taylor, another Glasgow School member, also used designs with shallow carving centrally positioned on symmetrical pieces. Rorimer's side chairs with tapered backs are also characteristic of this style.[24]

Homer Johnson, a client and friend, commissioned many pieces of furniture from Rorimer between 1903 and 1930. The lines of an oak chair and a desk dating from circa 1913 were influenced by the Glasgow School and European Art Nouveau. The semicircular cutout of the chair splat was influenced by the former, and the relief carving by the latter. The desk is a typical Arts and Crafts design, and its feet are similar to designs used by Arthur and Lucia Mathews and architect-designer Arthur Heygate Macmurdo.[25]

About 1903 Rorimer created a bedroom set using Egyptian motifs. Egyptiennerie, the fashion for decorative motifs derived from ancient Egyptian symbols, hieroglyphics, and architectural ornament, had flourished in the eighteenth century and found its way into French, Italian, and English Neoclassical design. Throughout the nineteenth century, romanticized versions of Egyptian forms and symbols influenced American furniture designs. But Howard Carter's discovery of the tomb of Thutmose IV in 1903 directed renewed attention toward the archaeologically correct furniture[26] of which Rorimer became an exponent.

For Johnson's bedroom set Rorimer used low-relief stylized carving on top of the headboard, footboard, and the cheval glass. The wedge-shaped sunray be tween each post and rectilinear head and footboard continues the motif, as do the lotus buds on the table legs and papyrus flowers on table and chair feet. The tapering vertical lines—a pylon temple shape—of the mirror, bed, and chair also contribute to the Egyptian appearance, while diagonal lattice-work braces on table and chair stretchers duplicate those found on Egyptian furniture.

Exoticism must have appealed to Johnson, because Rorimer made another bedroom set for Johnson's young son Philip, circa 1913, whose design was inspired by Far Eastern cultures. This cinnabar and black chinoiserie bed, desk, chair, cabinet, and mirror were modeled after a French prototype. Chinoiserie of this type relied on a variety of japanning techniques in imitation of lacquer. It had been popular in America in the eighteenth century and again following the Philadelphia Centennial Exhibition in 1876. Rorimer's c. 1913 version was unusual for its day but presaged the craze for Chinese-style lacquer

Chinoiserie cabinet and part of a bedroom suite made for Homer Johnson's son Philip in 1913. *Photo by David M. Thum. Mr. Bourne Dempsey collection.*

in the 1920s, which included furniture styles that were less Chinese than Rorimer's.[27]

Style is usually cyclical, and what makes an old style seem new is the timing of its reintroduction: even revolutionary Art Moderne designs were based on the historic precedents of neoclassicism. Although Rorimer's innovative designs were sometimes little more than new versions of old styles, his timing made them seem fresh. He introduced his own Arts and Crafts furniture to Cleveland just as top designers were introducing their most modern Arts and Crafts pieces in New York, Illinois, and California. Chinoiserie was not new, but Rorimer's cinnabar and black version was uncommon in 1913, as had been the green painted Egyptiennerie set ten years earlier. Rorimer was no copyist. He studied history and traveled often to European centers of design activity. Each custom-made piece of furniture synthesized Rorimer's understanding of good design, unencumbered by geographic or chronological limits.

Shaker Heights alone could have supported Rorimer's business, yet residents in other suburbs clamored for his interior designs and furnishings.[28] One of the finest Rorimer-Brooks Shaker Heights interiors dates from 1928. It remained intact until 1984, when the owner sold the house. Some of the furnishings remain in the Shaker Heights use; others are in the new residence of the owner. Cuyahoga County Archives photographed the home as a historic document prior to the sale. The paneling on the living room walls has a carved floral motif (similar to that on the built-in cabinets at Bigsbluff) that is repeated on the carved marble of the fireplace and, to a lesser extent, on the andirons. The same detail is used on a living room table.

Rorimer also provided other richly carved tables for the living room and several seating pieces. A round cane-backed chair is a good example of the historic hybridizations for which Rorimer became known. It is entirely of mahogany, the wood of choice in the eighteenth and early nineteenth centuries. The turned legs, Spanish feet, and scroll-carved stretcher are late seventeenth-century William and Mary elements, while the circular back is a late eighteenth-century Robert Adam design, and the seat and arms are Neoclassical features of about 1800. What Rorimer did in this William and Mary-Adam style chair was to combine features from some of the finest historic styles into one piece. Another explanation is that he designed a totally new chair based on what several noncontemporary designers might have done separately in the past. Rather than make a copy, Rorimer created a fresh and aesthetically pleasing object that reflected his firm understanding and enjoyment of past styles.

Even though most of the Rorimer furniture from the Shaker Heights home is now in a new context, it fits well in the new setting. A pair of brightly painted console tables in the Adam style, which grace the living room, have every available smooth surface decorated with acanthus leaf scrolls, bellflowers, figures, and paterae. Another pair of painted console tables are attached to facing walls of the dining room. Carved and painted supports are single-leg hoofed scrolls. Flowers bordering the richly grained marble tops create an effect that is reminiscent of the exuberant mixing of materials for Italian Baroque tables that have bold three-dimensional carving, brightly colored painting, marble, and gilded gesso. Rorimer's tables, although not in Baroque style, display all but the gilded gesso.

Rorimer chose to embellish even relatively simple side chairs with floral painting, and for several he used gold paint to accent the carving. Given that all of this furniture was commissioned, designed, and crafted at about the same time and was intended to coordinate with other pieces, the designs of tables, chests, and chairs are surprisingly varied.

Outside of furniture in Rorimer's family, the pieces designed for this Shaker Heights home are probably the best single dated collection of Rorimer furniture in existence. Its assortment of styles and diversity of carving and painting

Entrance and hall view of balcony of Shaker Heights home completed in 1928.
Photo by David Thum, Cuyahoga County Archives. Courtesy of the Western Reserve His-
torical Society, Cleveland, and Miss G. G. Peckham.

Kitchen of same Shaker Heights home done entirely by Rorimer-Brooks in 1928. *Photo by David Thum, Cuyahoga County Archives. Courtesy of the Western Reserve Historical Society, Cleveland, and Miss G. G. Peckham.*

provides an overview of what the company produced. The only category that is noticeably absent, besides Victorian (which he did not produce), is twentieth-century modern. This was a personal favorite of Rorimer's, but since he did not believe in imposing his taste on others, his most modern work was usually produced for his own consumption.

Rorimer resided at the Wade Park Manor in Cleveland's cultural center, University Circle. He kept these suites, but stayed only during the winter months after he designed and built a summer home for his family in 1928 on the tree-lined and hilly property surrounding Bigsbluff. He also designed it as a place for entertaining, in which the first floor is one great room with a few steps separating the dining area from the living room. The entire space can be

105

viewed from any vantage point, which conveys spaciousness and visual continuity. The house was in the woods, and it was secluded, so Louis and Edith Rorimer supplied maps along with invitations to guests.[29]

Rorimer built his house of sandstone quarried from the property. Its natural garden setting conveys Rorimer's desire to have his house show "that someone lives here who appreciates the natural beauty of the place."[30] Ferns and mossy rocks edge the trails of white sand laid between trees and boulders. Rorimer's personal "pastoral ideal" was what historian Leo Marx has identified as a middle ground: "Living in an oasis of rural pleasure, he enjoys the best of both worlds—the sophisticated order of art and the simple spontaneity of nature."[31] Rorimer integrated the best of his two worlds: his own artistic creations/collections and nature's harmonious wooded landscape. The twentieth-century world in which he worked was more than an hour's drive away. Rorimer never learned to drive. He made the transition from the pastoral world to the workaday one in the back seat of a chauffeured touring car, always a Packard.

Rorimer was in love with beauty, and he found it in nature, in art, and in technology. The appearance and appropriateness of people's surroundings seriously concerned him, thus that of his own personal environment became a special project. Since he could have created and produced any home interior imaginable, what he selected for his country summer home is an accurate index of his taste in the late 1920s. The first floor rooms resemble those by avant-garde Austrian and German architects, especially those associated with the Wiener Werkstätte.[32] Rorimer incorporated the feeling of these modern Viennese styles into the living and dining areas. White plaster walls, high vaulted ceilings with large dark beams and plank flooring provided the backdrop, while large windows offered dramatic views from both living and dining room. Rorimer self-consciously used this as an opportunity to incorporate the outdoor views with his interior design. The boldly colored hand-painted ceiling moldings, door casings, and beams blended Austrian-German and Scandinavian folk designs and were similar to elements used in Art Deco furnishings.[33] Because swans were a Rorimer emblem,[34] a swan was painted above a dining room door (and were elements of exterior iron balconies). Painted figural, floral, and geometric designs decorated the dining room furniture, and paint highlighted the carved designs of the dining table. A handsome piece of furniture is the large sideboard in the dining room, which has low relief and pierced foliate carving. The sideboard has a distinctly Northern European flavor, the result of Rorimer's Scandinavian travel.

Upstairs are the private family spaces. These rooms are separate and smaller and, except for a terraced ceiling, the architecture is less important. The focus is the furniture. Two bedrooms are filled with two different types of Art Deco painted furniture accented by Wiener Werkstätte accessories. One bedroom set is painted turquoise: twin beds, a dresser with detached hexagonal mirror, a vanity with attached arched mirror, a desk-and-bookcase, a chaise, a side chair, and a nightstand-bookcase. The other, off-white, set has twin beds,

Rorimer's dining table and chairs on the carpet he designed for his summer home in 1928. *Photo by author, private collection.*

a dresser, a writing desk, a side chair, a bench, a nightstand, a bookcase, a shelved cabinet, and a three-section mirrored vanity.

The absolutely modern design of both sets was directly influenced by the Paris Exposition. When Rorimer returned from Paris, he lectured and gave interviews about the new style. He even featured photographs of Art Moderne pieces in advertisements, yet few of his residential clients were ready to accept the style.[35] Rorimer was ready. For his summer home he designed two modern painted bedroom sets. On the off-white set, the three-tiered head and footboards, in a two-toned rectangular abstract design like a city skyline of skyscrapers, is a motif employed by other modern designers such as Paul Frankl, while silver leaf—another Frankl favorite[36]—in high-tech sculptural motifs disguise the legs. At the center of the headboards, frosted Lalique-like light covers soften the small reading lights installed onto the painted wood surface. The vanity bench has an Art Moderne stylized plant in silver leaf and abstract carved concentric quarter-circles where the top joins the sides. These embellishments enhanced an already modern design.

107

Art Deco vanity with mirror and bench. Rorimer designed two Art Deco bed-room suites for his summer home in 1928 shortly after returning from the Paris Exposition. (Vanity, H. 72-1/2″, W. 53-1/2″, D. 12″; bench with silver leaf on carving, H. 18″, W. 20″, D. 12-1/2″.) *Photo by Erik Liu, private collection.*

An extraordinary example of Art Moderne is a table that Rorimer personally designed and had executed at his studios out of circassian walnut, walnut, oak, maple, ebonized and silvered wood, aluminum, and brass-plated metal. It was originally part of an ensemble made for Rorimer's son James and daughter Louise in their New York apartment. The unusual proportions (90-1/2 inches wide opened, 50 inches wide closed, and 28 inches deep) were designed to fit into a small dining alcove, yet when fully extended with leaves, it seats eight.

This table was recently featured in an exhibition of some of the best American work produced in the late 1920s. Since Manhattan was then America's style center, all of these pieces were either made in Manhattan or by designers who were active there. Karen Davies, author of the exhibition catalog, places Rorimer's table in the section entitled "Using the Past," in which the objects are of modern design yet integrate historical influence. Rorimer's influence, as with many French Art Moderne designs, was Neoclassical. Use of a U-shaped support on a pedestal base was common on Empire tables. Although Rorimer would have justified having borrowed from the French as "respect for the usefulness of the past," Davies viewed it as something less than daring when she wrote, "This retrospective eclecticism in both conservative and progressive circles indicates a lack of confidence in contemporary American culture as a source of artistic inspiration."[37]

Davies is correct in pointing out the table's French Neoclassical inspiration. Whether or not this was due to a lack of confidence in contemporary American culture or to admiration for French design is an open question. Regardless of its source of inspiration, the table is an exceptional piece of furniture in both design and craftsmanship. Given the date of 1927, Davies may be unfair in her judgment, since the only major modern design event up until that time was the Paris Exposition just two years earlier. AUDAC had not yet been formed. Rorimer's table was both historically inspired and extremely modern—not a contradiction, but representative of a transitional phase in modern design.

The French-inspired phase of American modern design was a necessary transition between traditional and new American modern designs that were beginning to develop. Examples of Franco-American Art Moderne furniture were featured in *Good Furniture Magazine* in articles from 1926 to 1929.[38] In October 1927 it was observed that little modern furniture was being made in America. "American manufacturers are by no means bold adventurers as far as art moderne furniture is concerned." The explanation was economic. "That more manufacturers have not taken up the modern style can be accounted for, no doubt, by the fact that they have a steady demand for their own traditional styles, and deviation from the established routine would mean a considerable interruption to an already successful manufacturing policy."[39] W. Frank Purdy, writing for *Arts and Decoration* in 1920, blamed the manufacturers for failing to stimulate and satisfy the taste of the American public. These manufacturers had the ability, he believed, to successfully develop a national industrial art and to boost the public's confidence in American talent.[40] Most of the examples featured in the *Good Furniture* article are of French inspiration, but a few more "extreme modernist" designs by Kem Weber and J. B. Peters are illustrated. These designs exemplify the American talent of which Purdy and others spoke.

Franco-American Art Moderne proved to be a brief transition in the evolution of American modernism. In the 1930s designers pursued a clean-lined style that consciously avoided ornament, foreign influence, and the past. Rorimer created some of his most modern designs while a member of AUDAC, as demonstrated in an upholstered chair and lamp-table-bookcase made for the Pinehurst, North Carolina, home of Homer Johnson. Other AUDAC members designed the accompanying furniture and accessories for Johnson, and they represent some of the most radical and high-style American designs to date. Two nearly identical Rorimer pieces designed for Mr. and Mrs. John B. Dempsey of Bratenahl, Ohio, in 1929, were given to the Western Reserve Historical Society in Cleveland, where they are on exhibit. Although the chair was recently reupholstered, the fabric dates from the late 1920s and probably was carried by Rorimer-Brooks at the time, as evidenced by the one surviving book of fabric samples. The green and silver leaf dentil-patterned chair base is similar to that found on pieces by Frankl and by Hugo Gnam, Jr.[41]

Frankl once posited, "The history of civilization is recapitulated in the evolution of the chair. A whole philosophy lies concealed in the act of sitting." Since function is primary, "the unwary designer who sets for himself the goal of revolutionizing the chair usually falls into a trap."[42] Comfort, a particular aspect of function, was to be a high priority for modern design. In the past, Rorimer explained in an interview, "were hard, bleak times. Their chairs were mostly stiff and straight; it didn't matter that they were uncomfortable because the early Colonials didn't have time to sit in them. We have become a race of loungers. We have more time away from work. Our chairs, to be right according to this new mode of living, should be comfortable to lounge in indefinitely."[43] Rorimer applied these tenets in his chair. Its loose cushions and the flat surfaces covered with padded fabrics provide comfort in addition to a statement of fashion.

Modern designs of the 1920s and 1930s are no longer revolutionary because, contrary to the predictions of Rorimer's contemporaries, they were not a passing fad. American modernism by AUDAC members was only the preview of a revolution in American furniture design that occured in the 1950s. But until then, resistance persisted and modernism was found mostly in department stores and jewelry, perfume, and dress shops. Most American homes were still furnished in traditional styles, and leading magazines devoted to decorating did not promote the modern style. Even in the late 1940s the most significant American market was for seventeenth- and eighteenth-century reproductions and adaptations.[44]

According to author Cara Greenburg, "The early 1950s was not the first time modern furniture had been offered to the American public, but it was the first time that they lined up around the block to buy it."[45] The style called Modern had been in existence for more than two decades but had been neither

Modern living room designed for Homer Johnson's home in Pinehurst, North Carolina, in 1929. Rorimer's wood, metal, silver leaf, and upholstered armchair and painted wood table are featured with furnishings by some of America's most modern designers and members of AUDAC. *Photo by Eddy's Studio. Courtesy of Mrs. John B. Dempsey.*

The handwritten notes on the back of the photo read:

Pearl-gray heavy chenille carpet
White walls and ceiling
Black woodwork
Vermillion red (flame red) satin
  curtains
Furniture frames—black and silver
  leaf or aluminum
Desk vermillion lacquer with silver-
  leaf drawers and heavy mirror
  glass top
Cornices aluminum
Fire-place trim and book-case trim
  aluminum stripping

Upholstery—
  Silver and black on aluminum
    pieces
  Large arm-chair red and gray dia-
    mond figure
  Small [ditto] red—
  Couch—blue
  Pillows: black and red, and
    chartreuse yellow
  Wall Hangings—black and gray
    and silver

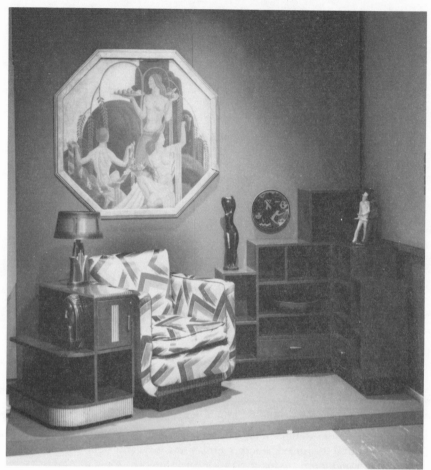

Armchair, lamp table, and "skyscraper" bookcase designed for Mr. and Mrs. John B. Dempsey of Bratenahl, Ohio, in 1929, now on display at the Western Reserve Historical Society, Cleveland. *Courtesy of the Western Reserve Historical Society, Cleveland.*

accessible nor acceptable to the consumer. Even Rorimer once complained, "Why I was looking at the designs for a built-in couch in one of those modernist rooms the other day. It looked fine. It was marvelous to lie in. But you couldn't sit on it in comfort to save your life. It was too deep. Nothing to lean back against."[46] When Rorimer and the AUDAC designers introduced both functional cleaned-lined Bauhaus-inspired furniture and exotic veneered Franco-American Art Moderne pieces, the depression made their already high cost prohibitive. Since Rorimer-Brooks designed relatively few of these modern pieces, there was little adverse impact on the company. Conditions of the depression demanded an institutionalized style of modernism, which was much cheaper to produce than the radical designer furniture. In addition, conserva-tism prevailed in middle America, the location of the very audience for which the modern style was intended. The "Golden Age of American Design" was unknown to the average American. The average prewar home was furnished with "Grand Rapids borax," a contemporary term for ill-designed and poorly constructed mass-market furniture that substituted applied motifs and compli-cated carving to mask total lack of understanding of the interrelationship of form and function.[47] Had history repeated itself?

During the pioneering years of modernism, the Chicago World's Fair of 1933 and 1934 featured the most advanced architecture and interiors in Amer-ica. Nevertheless, several of the rooms illustrated in *A Century of Progress: Homes and Furnishings* were in bland generic traditional styles. About half of the illustrations displayed mass-produced Thirties Modern designs, while a small percentage were radical with tubular steel tables, sofas, and chairs.[48]

In 1939 the New York World's Fair "set the stage for the postwar success of modern furniture by instilling in people a fantasy they would later try to live out by furnishing their homes in a futuristic way."[49] But in 1940 there was a brief regression to mid-nineteenth-century romanticism in which *House and Garden* featured a room that seemed a "satire of Victorian interiors." One au-thor writes, "By 1940, the visionary intensity with which modernity had been invoked by Bel Geddes early in the decade needed to be redirected toward the preparation for war."[50] After the war, the demand for machine-made mass-produced furniture was great. In fact, anything that referred to machines was venerated.

Design was also a reflection of economic and social changes that engen-dered lightness and mobility in furniture.[51] This trend had been anticipated in the early 1930s by the AUDAC designers. So-called skyscraper furniture, which had been based on the right angle and the unadorned plane, evolved into the standard design for storage pieces from the 1950s onward. Bauhaus designs had not been well received, partly because their introduction had been prema-ture. The 1950s adoration of the machine provided a more hospitable climate. Had Rorimer lived into the 1950s, he undoubtedly would have participated in that "golden age" of American furniture.

Rorimer-Brooks was, at least until Rorimer's death in 1939, the finest inte-rior design studio between New York and Chicago. Even if one judges it only on Rorimer's use of historically inspired designs and antiques, he was success-ful. Yet Rorimer once confessed to a friend, "I wish I could get rid of all this and have a little studio where I could model and carve and just play at my art."[52]

The extent of Rorimer's talent and vision went beyond furnishing homes with traditional objects. He was a modernist with a conservative clientele. The play between modern and traditional design is one that has had countless ver-sions throughout history, and design that consciously broke from its past was at one point modern. In America, Arts and Crafts and, to a lesser extent, Art Nouveau designs were one stage for modernism, and Rorimer was one of its players. Following the 1925 Paris Exposition, Art Moderne, another stage on

113

which Rorimer played, was transformed into American modernism, and that was a severe break with the past accompanied by cultural and technological changes. Rorimer, although a product of his times, recognized the rapidity with which these scenes were changing. In the light of all of the advances and declines in furniture design and production since the 1930s, Rorimer played the role of pioneer modernist with finesse and élan. His most advanced ideas did not rely upon historic precedents but became precedents for designs that followed. His knowledge and appreciation of the past and his insistence upon quality of materials and craftsmanship were significant elements in his more conventional designs. He was an artist and a connoisseur whose interpretive talents for recognizing and creating order and beauty were timeless.

APPENDIX A
Rorimer Clients

The following list, taken from the handwritten "Shop Detail Book," indicates names of both commercial and residential clients from 1929 through the 1930s. Only entries that appear more than once in the book are included.

1929

Bishop
Boston Statler
Mrs. W. N. Brewer
Buffalo Statler
Chesapeake and Ohio Railroad
Cleveland Museum of Art
Cleveland Statler
Cleveland Terminal Co.
Cleveland Trust
Colonade Restaurant, Co.
Daisy Hill Farm
Mrs. A. F. Davis
Mrs. C. S. Eaton
Mrs. D. Ford
Alfred Fritzche
F. W. Gehring
E. B. Green
Hotel Statler Club
Jenks
Jewish Orphan Home
Justin Sholes
Koppers Barber Shop and Bldg.
E. J. Kulas, Republic & Midland Steel
Harry Lynch
Midday Club
Moreland Courts Apartments

Osborn
Shaker Store
Milton Statler
10th Floor Club
W. G. Wilson
Wooster College

1930

Amshe Chesed Congregation
Baldwin
Blair
Blau
Builders Exchange Club
Church of the Covenant
The Country Club
Daisy Hill Farm
Detroit Colonade
Domino
Electrolux
J. Farden
W. E. Goff
Greenbrier Hotel and Resort
L. H. Hays
Hirsch Shop
Hirsch Tayloring Co.
David Johnson (David T. Johnston)

Woods King
Kleinman
Knutsen
Lake Forest Country Club
Lakeside Hospital
Leader Building
McKetterick
Mescho
Miles
Albert Mills
Mudler
National Town and Country Club
Oakwood Country Club
Plain Dealer
G. H. Quayle
R. C. A. Radiotron
George M. Rogers
H. C. Royal
St. Lukes Hospital
Schemck
Sherwin Williams
P. L. Small
Society of Steel
Trinkmen
Van Sweringen
Wilson Office
Mrs. W. Withington
Wolfe

1931

Boston Square Hotel
Hotel Cleveland
Hanna
Hobby Horse Farms
National City Bank
St. Pauls
Dr. John Tucker

1932

Addressograph
Appel
Brevailier
Daley

Joseph
Rosenblum
Stearn
Snyder

1933

Cleveland Electric Illuminating Co.
Crawford
Cunningham
Keppel
Marcus
Nela Park
Stanley
Stock
Wooster College
Zimmerman

1934

Detroit Statler
Higgens
Medusa C. Co.

1935

Burke
Duncan
Greenwald
May
McIntosh
Morgan
Newbury
Rohrheimer
Westheimer

1936

Black
Collins
D. A. C.
Geismer
Haas
Weisman

116

1937

Blossom
Evans
Fred Frankel
Gundelfinger
Metropolitan Museum of Art
Millikin
O'Neill
Poe
A. H. Sachs
St. Louis Statler
Scher
F. Tod

1938

W. J. Austin
Mayme T. Blum
Bernard F. Bernett
Boston Statler
J. C. Eberly
Farber Inc.
Friedheim
General Electric
Walter Gummins
Robert Hayes
Sam Levin
Dr. M. Luckiesh
Ralph Perkins
C. A. Quintrell
Robert Stecher

APPENDIX B
Inventory from Outside Suppliers, 1940

Because Rorimer-Brooks was a full-service interior design company and it did not have facilities for mass production, it was necessary to purchase some items not manufactured in its shops. The following list, which is divided according to categories of merchandise, indicates the names of companies and individuals who provided Rorimer-Brooks with inventory. The "Inventory Book" is for the year 1940, and it is not known how long these suppliers had been dealing with Rorimer-Brooks.

The number following some names, such as (2), indicates the number of categories supplied by that individual or company.

Show Room

A. A. Adams (4)
Adams and Co.
American Art Association
Ashley-Kent
Baker Furniture
Barnard and Simonds
Samuel Buckley Co. Ltd. (5)
S. J. Campbell Co.
Century Furniture
Compaigne de Bronzes
Conant Ball Co.
Decorative Utilities Co.
Dillingham Mfg. Co.
Drexel Furniture
V. Dumont and Co.—France (5)
Fine Arts
Fry and Co.—England
Edward Garrett Inc.
Grand Rapids Upholstery Co.
Heywook Wakefield
Houghton Studios

Albert Hubert—France (4)
Robert W. Irwin
Kaplan Furniture Co.
Williams Kimp
Kittenger Company
J. W. Lamb
Lifton Furniture Co.
Manufacturede Sigia (2)
Jose Maragas (4)
B. L. Marble Chair Co.
Marble and Shattuck Chair Co.
Harry Meyers
Herman Miller Furniture
Montlor
Murray Furniture Co.
Nahon Co.
Northern Picture Frame Co. (2)
O. Olivotti Co. (2)
Orsenigo Company
Paallman Co.
Palmer and Embury Mfg. Co.
Margaret Palmer (4)
Premier Furniture

Restall, Brown, & Glennell
Shaw Furniture Co.
Barnard Simonds
Elgin A. Simonds
Sligh Furniture Co.
W. and J. Sloane Co. (2)
Societe Glaenzer (2)
R. J. Stanek (4)
F. Tibbenham
Vegroda (2)
Wainswright—England
J. W. Whitlock Co.
John Widdicomb Co.
Cooper Williams

Pictures and Mirrors

A. A. Adams (4)
Edward T. Bacon
Bon Marche—Paris
Samuel Buckley Co. Ltd. (5)
Buntman Furniture
Harry Calloway (also Harry Galloway, W. H. S. Lloyd)
V. Dumont and Co. (5)
Feika Imports
Wm. S. French and Co.
Albert Hubert (4)
International Frame and Picture Co.
Rudolph Lesch Fine Arts
Jose Maragas (4)
Philip Moore and Son
F. J. Newcomb and Son
Northern Picture Frame Co. (2)
E. Richter
Mrs. Louis Rorimer, consignor
Max Sinz—Germany
W. and J. Sloane Co. (2)
F. J. Stanek
R. J. Stanek—Vienna (4)
Paul B. Victorius
Vixseboxse Galleries
Helen Zolin

Ornaments

A. A. Adams (4)

Art Lamp Co.
Baker Inc.
Baltimore Clipper C. (C. J. White, Agent)
Fred Benedict
Samuel Buckley Co. Ltd. (5)
Cantigalli, Adams, Lowe, and Co.
Carbone Co.
L. Chelvux
China Overseas (2)
City of Hankow Tallel Co.
V. Dumont and Co. (5)
Orin Elsey
Eton Paper Co.
Edward J. Farmer
Feika Imports
Fujita & Co.—San Francisco
Gerard
Glaenzer-Gilson and Co. (2)
Goldy Studios
Guidance and Bruno (2)
Guinard
Gustavsberg—Stockholm
Charles Hall Inc. (2)
Hippolyte Guinarde
Howe Leather Products
Albert Hubert (4)
Levins and Ling
Little, Jones, and Co. (2)
Long Sang Ti (2)
Lorenzo, Rubelli, and Fige
R. H. Macy
Manufacture de Sigia (2)
Jose Maragas (4)
Jean Mesker
Jean Mesku—Morocco
Alfred (Orlick)
Margaret Palmer—Spain (4)
Panama Exposition
Pearson Page
Pierson and Page
Pilley and Co. Ltd.—England
George Rance
Russian Antique Shop
Mrs. John Rust, consignor
Saito
G. Schroeder
Smith Metal Arts Co.
Southern Sea Shops

Taube Co. (2)
William H. Tombs (2)
A. J. van Dugteren and Sons (2)
Wehner and Hartkopf
Wilson Shops—St. Louis

Fabric, Tapestry, and Rugs

Samuel Buckley Co. Ltd. (5)
R. Carillo and Co.
V. Dumont and Co. (5)
Gio Batta Trapolin
Glaenzer-Gilson and Co. (2)
Hegroda (?)
Hippolyte Guinard
Margaret Hochsinger
Kent Costikyan Co.
Jose Maragas (4)
Mountain Community
O. Olivotti Co. (2)
Margaret Palmer (4)
Salvadore
F. Schumacker and Co.
Max Sickerman
Societe Glaenzer (2)
R. J. Stanek (4)
J. H. Thorpe
Vegroda (2)
Virginia Craftsmen

Lamps and Shades

A. A. Adams (4)
Edward Alden
Michael Bluhm
Samuel Buckley Co. Ltd. (5)
Chaska Studios

China Overseas (2)
Colonial Premier Co.
Frederick Cooper
V. Dumont and Co. (5)
E. Elson
Herbert Elson
Erle
Goody Lamp Co.
H. Leo Gould
Guidance and Bruno (2)
Charles Hall Inc. (2)
Halle Bros. Co.
Albert Hubert (4)
Karl Jaunsarin
A. N. Khouri and Bros.
Lightolier
Little, Jones and Co. (2)
Long Sang Ti (2)
Miles Studios
Mutual Sunset Lamp Mfg. Co.
Northern Ohio Plating
Margaret Palmer (4)
Robert Phillips Co.
Plaza Studios
E. Poisell
P. J. Rivers Sr.
Shade Studios
Soenda Co.
Joseph Stahl
R. J. Stanek (4)
Sterling Bronze Co.
Sydenham Studio
Taube Co. (2)
William H. Tombs (2)
A. J. van Dugteren and Sons (2)
E. G. Wehner
Whitelow Studio
Helen Wood Studios
Russel Wright

◆§♯❧

NOTES

INTRODUCTION

1. Carlton Matson, "Louis Rorimer—Businessman of Art," *Cleveland Press*, Nov. 10, 1932, unpaginated clipping in Rorimer Archives, property of Mrs. James Rorimer. When Rorimer died in 1939, his son James collected samples of company records and other Rorimer-related materials and filed them. About 1950, when he moved to their summer home (called Bigsbluff), these papers were sealed in a Rorimer-Brooks desk, and they were not discovered until Memorial Day of 1986, when the desk door popped open. These papers have been designated the Rorimer Archives. See also Grace Kelly, "Art Museum Given Rorimer Memorial," *Cleveland Plain Dealer*, April 26, 1946, unpaginated clipping in Cleveland Museum of Art files: Ben Bassham, ed., *The Memories of an American Impressionist: Abel G. Warshawsky* (Kent, Ohio: Kent State University Press, 1980), p. 9; Robert Bordner, "Louis Rorimer Designs Modern Furniture," *Cleveland Plain Dealer*, Nov. 7, 1931, p. 5; "New Muse Leads Art Rebels Here," Unknown newspaper, Feb. 11, 1911, unpaginated clipping in Cleveland Institute of Art "Scrapbook," vol. 3, p. 55; "Louis Rorimer," *Cincinnati Enquirer*, Dec. 2, 1939, unpaginated clipping; "Louis Rorimer, 67, Artist, Decorator," *New York Times*, Dec. 1, 1939, obituary page; "Louis Rorimer is Dead at 67," *Cleveland Press* Nov. 30, 1939, p. 1.

2. Cleveland Chamber of Commerce, *Medals Awarded for Merit in Building 1917* (Cleveland: Chamber of Commerce, 1917), pp. 15 and 17.

CHAPTER 1. FOUNDATIONS

1. Although his family retained the original spelling of their name as Rohrheimer, Louis had his name legally changed to Rorimer in 1917 due to postwar anti-German sentiment plus a climate of anti-Semitism, following a period in which he spelled his name as Rorheimer. He is referred to throughout this book as Rorimer.

2. Each *Cleveland City Directory* from 1853 to 1888 lists Jacob Rohrheimer's tobacco business under "Rohrheimer" in the alphabetical listings. Tobacco, which supported Rorimer as a child and which he enjoyed in his pipe for many years, eventually contributed to his death, which was brought about by complications after a tracheotomy.

3. Sidney Vincent and Judah Rubenstein, *Merging Traditions: Jewish Life in Cleveland* (Cleveland: Western Reserve Historical Society and Jewish Community Federation of Cleveland, 1978), pp. 73, 81, and 93. The earliest evidence of Jews in Cleveland was 1836 (p. 77); Cleveland city directories list Rohrheimer's presidency from 1876 to 1882. The caption under his photograph on page 49 of Bing and Haas, eds., *The Temple 1850–1950* (Cleveland: The Temple), gives the dates as 1874–81 and 1882–84.

4. Carle Robbins, "Louis Rorimer—Three Dimensional Man," *Cleveland Bystander* 11, no. 50 (Dec. 14, 1929): 31–32.

5. Robbins, "Louis Rorimer," p. 32; at least 275 Americans had studied art in Munich between 1870 and 1885. According to Michael Quick, "The foreign art academies became major factors not only in lifting the quality of American art, but in shaping its character as well.... The vast majority of Americans chose between Paris and Munich." The number of Americans studying in Munich continued at the same level until the turn of the century. "By the 1890's hardly a single major artist had not studied abroad for a number of years" (Michael Quick, *Munich and American Realism in the 19th Century* [Sacramento: Crocker Art Gallery, 1978], pp. 22 and 23).

6. Edna Maria Clark, *Ohio Art and Artists* (Richmond: Garrett and Massie, 1932; reprint, Detroit: Gale Research, 1975), pp. 126, 439, 444, 462, 475, and 499; Louis Loeb, letter to Rorimer dated July 14, 1903, in Rorimer Archives; Bassham, *Memories of an American Impressionist*, p. 28.

7. Rorimer to Abe Stearn, July 12, 1892. Stearn, husband of Rorimer's older sister Bettie, resided on Case Avenue (East Fortieth Street), the street of fashionable Woodland-area homes in the 1880s and 1890s. Photos of both the exterior and interior of Stearn's home are reprinted in Vincent and Rubenstein, *Merging Traditions*, p. 106. His business, Stearn and Company, imported and dealt in fancy goods, toys, and wooden and willow ware (p. 89).

8. William Innes Homer, *Robert Henri and His Circle* (Ithaca, New York: Cornell University Press, 1969), pp. 40 and 131.

9. "New Muse Leads Art Rebels Here."

10. Bassham, *Memories of an American Impressionist*, pp. 138–39.

11. Oscar Lovell Triggs, *Chapters in the History of the Arts and Crafts Movement* (Chicago, 1902; reprint, New York: Arno, 1979).

12. Isabelle Anscombe and Charlotte Gere, Arts and Crafts in Britain and America (London: Academy, 1978), p. 70.

13. Robert Judson Clark, ed., *The Arts and Crafts Movement in America 1876–1916* (Princeton, N.J.: Princeton Univ. Press, 1972), p. 58.

14. Triggs, *History of the Arts and Crafts Movement;* and Society of Arts and Crafts, *Handicraft, vol 1 and 2* (Boston: Society of Arts and Crafts, 1902–3).

15. Louis Rorimer, "Art in Relation to the Industries," abstract and paper dated May 15 in Rorimer Archives. According to an article, "The Cleveland Convention," in *American Magazine of Art* (July 1925, p. 348), Rorimer spoke on "Art and Industry." Therefore, the paper can be dated May 15, 1925.

16. Rorimer, "Art in Relation to the Industries," pp. 1, 2, and 8.

17. Louis Rohrheimer, "Art in the Home," in Autumn Social Minutes (Oct. 29, 1903) in *Cleveland Section, National Council of Jewish Women Records,* Western Reserve Historical Society (hereafter referred to as WRHS) Library, container 2, folder 3; French, "Head and Shoulders: Impressario of the Arts," *Parade,* Sept. 22, 1932, p. 13.

18. Werner Schweiger, *Wiener Werkstätte: Design in Vienna 1903–1932* (New York: Abbeville, 1984), pp. 5–8 and 12–23.

19. Andrew Probala, interview, May 29, 1985.

20. See for example, Gilian Naylor, *The Bauhaus* (London: Studio Vista, 1968); Frank Whitford, *Bauhaus* (London: Thames and Hudson, 1985).

21. Naylor, *Bauhaus,* p. 7.

22. The term *Art Deco* describes the predominantly French style seen at L'Exposition des Arts Décoratifs et Industriels Modernes in 1925. Although Art Deco is synonymous with costly and finely crafted Art Moderne, the term is also used to describe various derivations of the style produced through the 1930s; Bordner, "Louis Rorimer Designs Modern Furniture," p. 5.

23. Elizabith Aslin, *The Aesthetic Movement: Prelude to Art Nouveau* (London: Elek, 1969; reprint, New York: Excalibur, 1981), p. 175.

24. Charles Rennie Mackintosh, architect and modern designer, headed the Glasgow School around the turn of the century. Joseph Hoffman, modern designer, was a founder of the Wiener Werkstätte in 1903.

25. Bob Fillous, telephone interview, May 30, 1985.

26. French, "Head and Shoulders;" p. 12. Louise Rorimer Duskin, interview, Aug. 8, 1985; for discussions by Bing see Samuel Bing, *Artistic America, Tiffany Glass, and Art Nouveau* (Cambridge: MIT Press, 1970), pp. 213–51. Although most sources consider Bing's first name to be Samuel, according to authority Gabriel Weisberg, his first name was Siegfried. (Catherine Barnett, review of Bing's book, *Art and Antiques*, Nov. 1986, p. 109.)

27. French, "Head and Shoulders," p. 28.

28. Robbins, "Louis Rorimer," p. 32.

29. Dushkin, interview, Aug. 8, 1985; Probala, interview, May 29, 1985.

30. Dushkin, interview, Aug. 8, 1985; Probala, interview, May 29, 1985; French, "Head and Shoulders," p. 13.

31. Philippe Garner, *The Encyclopedia of Decorative Arts 1890–1940* (New York: Van Nostrand Reinhold, 1978), p. 80.

32. "Memorial Today to Honor Rorimer" *Cleveland Plain Dealer*, Dec. 1, 1939.

33. Dushkin, interview, Aug. 8, 1985.

34. French, "Head and Shoulders," p. 13. According to French, Norman Bel Geddes was one of Rorimer's students, but since Geddes attended the Cleveland School of Art only briefly in 1911 (Kenneth Reid, "Norman Bel Geddes, Master of Design" *Pencil Points,* Jan 1937, p. 3), there is little significance to this teacher-student relationship. However, Rorimer and Bel Geddes later became well acquainted (Mrs. James Rorimer, interview, May 28, 1986).

35. Robbins, "Louis Rorimer," p. 32.

36. Bassham, "Memories of an American Impressionist," p. 9.

37. Robbins, "Louis Rorimer," p. 33; Viktor Schreckengost, interview, May 6, 1985.

38. Schreckengost, interview, May 6, 1985.

39. Probala, interview, June 25, 1985.

40. French, "Head and Shoulders," p. 13; Wendy Kaplan, *The Art That Is Life: The Arts and Crafts Movement in America, 1875–1920* (Boston: Little, Brown, 1987), p. 272.

41. Cleveland Architectural Club, *Exhibition Catalogue* (Cleveland, 1909).

42. Rorimer, "Art in the Home." Two years later, the Weiner Werkstätte "Working Program" of Joseph Hoffman and Kolo Moser echoed Rorimer by stating: "In artistic terms, copper is just as valuable as precious metals, as far as we are concerned. . . . The worth of artistic work and of inspiration must be recognized and prized once again" (Schweiger, *Weiner Werkstätte*, p. 43).

43. Robbins, "Louis Rorimer," p. 32.

CHAPTER 2. CULTURE

1. Cleveland Architectural Club, *Exhibition Catalogues* (Cleveland, 1896 and 1897).

2. Cleveland Architectural Club, *Exhibition Catalogue* (Cleveland, 1900), p. 31.

3. Louis C. Tiffany and Frank Lloyd Wright also exhibited alongside Rorimer, suggesting that he knew these important American designers; Cleveland Architectural Club, *Exhibition Catalogue* (Cleveland, 1901).

4. Theodore Sizer to Rorimer, Dec. 22, 1925, Cleveland Museum of Art (hereafter referred to as CMA) records, Cleveland, Ohio. All correspondence between Rorimer and CMA staff members are from files in the office of the museum director.

5. Ibid.

6. Frederic Allen Whiting to Rorimer, June 1, 1920, CMA records.

7. Sizer to Rorimer, Jan. 17, 1925, CMA records.

8. Rorimer-Brooks estimate, Aug. 30, 1915, CMA records. Monk's cloth is "a coarse heavy fabric in basket weave made originally of worsted and used for monk's habits but now chiefly of cotton or linen and used for draperies" (*Webster's Ninth New Collegiate Dictionary*, s.v. "monk's cloth"). Whiting to Rorimer, June 21, 1918, CMA records. The dictionary defines holland as "a cotton or linen fabric in plain weave usually heavily sized or glazed and used for window shades, bookbinding, and clothing" (*Webster's Ninth New Collegiate Dictionary*, s.v. "holland").

9. Staff member to William Green, Nov. 15, 1923, CMA records.

10. William Millikin to Rorimer, Jan. 28, 1936, CMA records.

11. Henry Sayles Francis to Rorimer, Feb. 5, 1936, CMA records.

12. *Bulletin of the Cleveland Museum of Art* 6 (June 1919).

13. *Bulletin of the Cleveland Museum of Art* 7 (June 1920).

14. *Bulletin of the Cleveland Museum of Art* 9 (May 1922); 10 (May 1923); 11 (May 1924); 12 (May 1925); 13 (May 1926); 15 (May 1928). Two of Rorimer's student sketchbooks are in the Rorimer Archives, and photocopies are at the Western Reserve Historical Society.

15. Robbins, "Louis Rorimer," p. 35.

16. "In Memoriam—Louis Rorimer," *Bulletin of the Cleveland Museum of Art* (Feb. 1940), p. 16.

17. Cleveland Institute of Art, list of past officers in library manuscript collection; Robbins, "Louis Rorimer," p. 34.

18. American Federation of Arts, *American Art Annual: 1934*, vol. 30 (Washington D.C.: American Federation of Arts, 1935); and membership cards belonging to Rorimer, 1937 to 1939, in Rorimer Archives.

19. "Cleveland Arts Club, Cleveland, Ohio, Record Book 1913–1917," in manuscript collection of WRHS Library.

20. Cleveland Arts Club, flyer in folder at WRHS.

21. "Obituary." *Silhouette* (Cleveland, 1939), unpaginated, in Cleveland Museum of Art Library "artist files."

22. Ihna Thayer Frary, "Louis Rorimer 1872–1939," p. 3, eulogy delivered on Dec. 1939 at memorial service held at the home of Paul Feiss in Cleveland Heights. (Copy to be deposited at WRHS.) Feiss was board chairman of Joseph and Feiss Company, a manufacturer of women's clothing.

23. Rorimer to Abe Stearn, Dec. 3, 1891, and July 12, 1892, in Rorimer Archives; Rorimer-Brooks, "Inventory Book," 1939; Mrs. James Rorimer, interview, June 6, 1986.

24. Rowfant Club history in "A Register of its Records (1891–1973)," manuscript processed by Catherine Stover in 1973; manuscript collection of WRHS Library.

25. Charles S. Brooks, "The Cleveland Play House," *Theatre Arts Monthly,* Aug. 1926, p. 516.

26. Frederic McConnell, "The Cleveland Playhouse," *Architectural Record* 62 (Aug. 1927): 93.

27. Matson, "Louis Rorimer," unpaginated.

28. French, "Head and Shoulders," p. 28.

29. Quoted in Winifred Willson, "Beautiful Antique and Modern House Furnishings," *Arts and Decoration*, Feb. 1925, p. 48.

30. Photograph in Rorimer archives.

31. "Decorative Artists Form Union," *Architectural Record*, Aug. 1928, p. 164; according to AUDAC, membership included "the most outstanding men and women in the decorative arts and architecture, who are giving our environment a new and appropriate appearance" (American Union of Decorative Artists and Craftsmen, *AUDAC Exhibition* [New York: Brooklyn Museum, 1931]).

32. Donald McGregor, "AUDAC in Brooklyn," *Good Furniture and Decoration,* June 1931; "The AUDAC Exhibition," *Brooklyn Museum Quarterly* 18 (July 1931): 93–97; Matson, "Louis Rorimer."

33. Blanch Naylor, "American Design Progress," *Design* 33 (Sept. 1931): 83.

34. Lewis Mumford, "Cuture and Machine Art," in R. L. Leonard and C. A. Glassgold, eds., *Annual of American Design 1931* (New York: Ives Washburn, 1930), pp. 9 and 10.

35. Quoted in Ethel Pool, "Louis Rorimer Finds New Art Note in Paris Exhibit," *Country Club News*, Aug. 25, 1925, p. 34.

36. Paul Frankl, "The Home of Yesterday, Today, and Tomorrow," in Leonard and Glassgold, *Annual of American Design 1931*, p. 26.

37. See for example, Bordner, "Louis Rorimer Designs Modern Furniture."

38. Frankl, "Home of Yesterday, Today, and Tomorrow," p. 26.

39. Quoted in Pool, "Louis Rorimer Finds New Art Note," p. 34.

40. Arthur Pulos, *American Design Ethic: A History of Industrial Design* (Cambridge: MIT Press, 1983), p. 336; American Federation of Arts, *American Art Annual: 1932*, vol. 29 (Washington D.C.: American Federation of Arts, 1933), p. 221.

41. Probala, interview, May 29, 1985; Schreckengost, interview, May 6, 1985.

42. American Society of Interior Designers, "The Past as Prologue: The First 50 Years," *Annual Report 1980* (New York: ASID, 1981), p. 5; Matson, "Louis Rorimer—Businessman of Art."

43. "Interior Designers Organize," *Cleveland Bystander*, Nov. 14, 1931, p. 19; American Federation of Arts, *American Art Annual: 1934*, pp. 48–49.

44. Probala, interview, May 29, 1985; ASID, *Annual Report, 1980*, p. 8.

45. Certificate, Nov. 2, 1899, in Rorimer Archives.

46. Rudolph Rosenthal and Helena Ratzka, *The Story of Modern Applied Art* (New York: Harper and Bros, 1948), p. 174. When interviewed by the *New York Times* in August of 1925, Rorimer also observed that America had no modern art ("Expects New Trend in Decorative Arts," *New York Times*, Aug. 16, 1925, p. 26, col. 1).

47. United States Department of Commerce, *Report of the Commission Appointed by the Secretary of Commerce to Visit and Report upon the International Exposition of Modern Decorative and Industrial Art in Paris 1925* (Washington, D.C.: U.S. Commerce Department, 1926), pp. 5 and 9; Edward L. Bernays, *Biography of an Idea: Memoirs of Public Relations Counsel Edward L. Bernays* (New York: Simon and Schuster, 1965), p. 309.

48. U.S. Dept. of Commerce, *Report of the Commission*, pp. 6 and 13.

49. "Mr. Rorimer's Appointment," *Cleveland Topics*, May 23, 1925, p. 24.

50. Quoted in Pool, "Louis Rorimer Finds New Art Notes," p. 33.

51. "Modern Decorative Arts from Paris at the Metropolitan Museum of Art," *American Magazine of Art*, April 1926, p. 174.

52. Quoted in Frary, "Louis Rorimer 1872–1939," p. 4.

53. See for example, Henry-Russell Hitchcock, Jr. "Some American Interiors in the Modern Style," *Architectural Record*, Sept. 1928, pp. 236, 238, and 241; Nellie C. Sanford, "Decorating in Art Moderne," *Good Furniture Magazine* 31, no. 5 (Nov. 1928): 241–45; "French Art Moderne Exposition in New York," *Good Furniture Magazine*, Sept. 1928, pp. 119–22.

54. William Lescaze to Rorimer, Dec. 20, 1934, in Rorimer Archives.

55. See for example, "Art Moderne for a Conservative Clientele," *Good Furniture Magazine*, Sept. 1928, pp. 131–33.

56. Quoted in Pool, "Louis Rorimer Finds New Art Notes," pp. 33 and 34.

57. "Expects New Trend," p. 26, col. 1.

58. Martin Greif, *Depression Modern: The Thirties Style in America* (New York: Universe Books, 1975), pp. 28, 31, and 36.

59. "Expects New Trend," p. 26, col. 1.

60. Bordner, "Louis Rorimer Designs Modern Furniture," p. 5.

61. Frary, "Louis Rorimer 1872–1939," p. 3.

CHAPTER 3. THE COMPANY

1. Marshall B. Davidson and Elizabeth Stillinger, *The American Wing at the Metropolitan Museum of Art* (New York: Alfred A. Knopf, 1985), p. 190.

2. Wilson H. Faude, "Associated Artists and the American Renaissance in the Decorative Arts," in Ian Quimby, ed., *Winterthur Portfolio 10* (Charlottesville, Va.: Univ. Press of Virginia, 1975), p. 101.

3. Faude, "Associated Artists," p. 121; Robert Koch, *Louis C. Tiffany: Rebel in Glass*, updated 3d ed. (New York: Crown, 1982), p. 16.

4. Faude, "Associated Artists," pp. 102 and 128.

5. Koch, *Louis C. Tiffany*, p. 135.

6. Edith Wharton and Ogden Codman, Jr., *The Decoration of Houses* (New York: Scribner's, 1902; Reprint, New York: W. W. Norton, 1978); Allen Tate and C. Ray Smith, *Interior Design in the Twentieth Century* (New York: Harper and Row, 1986), pp. 242–43.

7. Erica Brown, *Sixty Years of Interior Design: The World of McMillen* (New York: Viking, 1982), p. 14; Tate and Smith, *Interior Design*, pp. 272–77.

8. Brown, *Sixty Years of Interior Design*, p. 15. Eleanor McMillen became Mrs. Brown in 1934.

9. Ibid., pp. 34 and 85.

10. *Cleveland Amusement Gazette*, Dec. 21, 1895, p. 29; French, "Head and Shoulders," pp. 12, 13, and 28; Rorimer's sketchbook from Toledo, Spain, dated Nov. 18, 1923, in Rorimer Archives; the "Minutes" of the Tefereth Israel Congregation of 1901 mention Rorimer as having designed a window; a silver tea set designed by Rorimer and labeled "Rokesley Shop" was given to his daughter Louise; silver jewelry designed by Rorimer was given to Louis Hays and now belongs to Rorimer's grandson Louis (Louis Rorimer II).

11. Richard Campen, "Louis Rorimer 1872–1939," unpublished paper written in August 1964 about the 2232 Euclid Avenue building and Rorimer. A photocopy was given to the author by Louis Rorimer II.

12. Campen, "Louis Rorimer," p. 3; French, "Head and Shoulders," p. 12; Probala, interview, May 29, 1985.

13. "Mrs. Joseph Joseph Dies: End is Written to Career of Unselfish Good Works," n.d.; "Mrs. Joseph Joseph," *Cincinnati Enquirer*, Nov. 25, 1949. Copies of clippings from the Library of the Cincinnati Historical Society were given to the author by Derek Ostergard.

Like Rorimer, Edith received European schooling during a four-year stay in Dresden and Brussels (Interview with Alan Geismer, grandson of Rorimer's sister Bettie, on Feb. 9, 1985). Edith's only association with Rorimer-Brooks was her advice and encouragement. They had two children, Louise and James, both of whom would become involved in the arts. As a young woman, Louise attended school in Paris before marrying concert violinist Samuel Dushkin. James eventually became director of the Metropolitan Museum of Art and married one of its librarians, Katherine Serrell. Edith frequently traveled to Europe with Rorimer or just with the children. Her brother Eli lived in Paris from 1922 until the Nazi occupation in 1940, which may have made long stays in Paris more convenient for them ("Businessman is Claimed in Death," *Cincinnati Enquirer*, Aug. 8, 1945, obituary). Eli was one of many relatives who fled from the Nazi regime. Some of Rorimer's relatives were killed in Germany, but Rorimer was successful in helping others to escape (Bella Rohrheimer letters, 1939–40, WRHS Library; and interview with Mrs. James Rorimer on June 6, 1986).

14. He has also been credited with forming the Kaynee Company, a well-known Cleveland manufacturer of boys' clothing. He stayed until 1914, and later became president of the Charles Eisenman Company. Prior to his partnership with Rorimer, Hays had worked in Eisenman's manufacturing department for two years (Campen, "Louis Rorimer," p. 3; *Cleveland* [Chicago: Lewis, 1918], p. 315).

15. Cleveland Playhouse (program?), undated, p. 15, Rorimer Archives; "Memorial Today."

16. *The Cleveland Manual Training School* (Cleveland, June 1899) in Ihna Thayer Frary, "Scrapbook," WRHS Library, container 3, folder I; Steven Fisher, "Ihna Thayer Frary: Register of His Papers 1895–1963 in the Western Reserve Historical Society" (Cleveland: WRHS Library, 1976); and Frary, "Scrapbook," container 3, folder II. Fisher processed the Frary papers and wrote an introduction.

17. *Cleveland City Directory* 1904.

18. French, "Head and Shoulders," p. 13.

19. Brooks Household Art Company, *The House Beautiful* (Cleveland: Brooks Household Art Company [1900]), unpaginated; Frary, "Scrapbook," container 3, folder 5. A list of Brooks's clients in 1905 can be found in *Art in Modern House Furnishing* ("Scrapbook," container 3, folder I).

20. L. H. Chapin, "A Fine Store" in Frary, "Scrapbook," container 3, folder II.

21. Magazine advertisements for Rorimer-Brooks are usually full or half-page and include photographs of furnishings (*Your Garden* [April 1927 to December 1930] was changed to *Your Garden and Home* in January 1931): *Your Garden:* July, Sept., and Nov. 1928; Jan., Feb., May, June, July, Sept., Oct., Nov., and Dec. 1929; all of 1930; *Your Garden and Home:* Jan., Feb., March, May, June, July, Aug., Sept., Oct., and Dec. 1931; Jan., Feb., March, April, June 1 and 15, 1932; Dec. 1935; Jan. 1936; *Country Club News:* Nov. and Dec. 1925; *Town and Country Club News:* Aug. 1925; Jan., April, May, Oct., and Nov. 1926; April, May, June, July, and Aug. 1927; April and June 1928;

Cleveland Bystander: Sept. 1 and 8, Nov. 3, Dec. 8 and 15, 1928; all of 1929; Jan. 25, 1930; *Cleveland Topics:* all of 1928, mostly full-page inside front cover.

22. *Your Garden,* Aug. 1930, inside front cover; *Cleveland Bystander,* Dec. 14, 1929, p. 30.

23. *Cleveland Bystander,* Dec. 14, 1929, p. 32; *Your Garden and Home,* Feb. 1932, p. 15; *Your Garden,* May 1929; *Your Garden,* Oct. 1929; Century Furniture Company, *Furniture as Interpreted by the Century Furniture Company* (Grand Rapids: Century Furniture, 1931), pp. 7 and 9.

24. *Your Garden,* March 1930.

25. *Your Garden,* Oct. 1931, p. 58; *Your Garden and Home,* Dec. 1931, p. 19.

26. Probala, interview, May 29, 1985. The photographs identified by Mr. Probala were taken over fifty years earlier, but he had worked closely with these individuals, so a high degree of accuracy is assumed. Ed Carome supplied the information about his father, Michele, in a telephone interview on June 5, 1985.

27. *Your Garden and Home,* July 1931, p. 23; *Your Garden and Home,* March 1931, inside front cover; *Your Garden and Home,* October 1931, p. 58.

28. "Rorimer-Brooks Itemization of Purchases Since 1935," for R. W. Scott, typescript, in author's possession. Probala, interview, May 25, 1985. Because only the employees' initials were used in the book, Probala has helped to identify several of these designers and salesmen. Salesmen include Louis Rorimer, Ray Warren Irvin, Monty Gormly (who later became Irvin's partner at Irvin and Company), William Kohler, Herbert Exley Cave, Robert Boone, Louise Thompson, Harry Lynch, [?] Westfall, [?] Koebler, and Phillip T. Hummel (Rorimer's personal secretary).

29. Phillip T. Hummel, interview, May 14, 1984. According to Andrew Probala (telephone interview on Sept. 24, 1986), Irvin opened branches on East Twelfth Street in the Chesterfield and at Eaton Square, a shopping mall that opened in Woodmere Village shortly before 1976. Soon after, all three locations closed at the same time.

30. Payroll sheets, Rorimer Archives; Probala, telephone interview, Sept. 24, 1986.

31. Probala interview, May 29, 1985.

32. United States Department of Commerce, Bureau of Census, *Historical Statistics of the United States: Colonial Times to 1970* (Washington, D.C.: Commerce Department 1975), charts on pp. 164, 166, 167, and 304.

33. Ibid., p. 167.

34. Ibid.; affidavit regarding stock in Rorimer-Brooks, 1933, in Rorimer Archives; payroll sheets, Rorimer Archives; Mrs. James Rorimer, interview, May 28, 1986.

35. Hummel, interview, May 14, 1984; Probala, interview, May 29, 1985.

36. Probala, interview, May 29, 1985.

37. See for example, letters to Rorimer from M. J. Goldschmit, Nov. 1 and Nov. 5, 1936; from William Lescaze, Jan. 21, 1937; from Otto Henks, Feb. 16, 1937; and from Morley Fletcher, March 8, 1939, all in Rorimer Archives.

38. Probala, interview, May 29, 1985.

39. Payroll sheets; sales report sheet, 1938, in Rorimer Archives; United States Board of Tax Appeals, "Docket No. 58850 Louis Rorimer, Petitioner v. Commissioner of Internal Revenue, Respondent," March 7, 1933, in Rorimer Archives.

40. Record sheets, 1939 and 1940, in Rorimer Archives.

41. Record sheets, 1939 and 1940; Record sheet, 1938, in Rorimer Archives. For most of the salesmen on both of the above lists, the "total salary and commission" figure is higher than that on the sheet entitled "salaries." Yet, for two salesmen, the reverse is true, and at present this cannot be accounted for.

42. Rorimer-Brooks, "Inventory Book," 1940, in Rorimer Archives.

43. Rorimer-Brooks, "Inventory Book," 1939, in Rorimer Archives.

44. Phil Hummel, telephone interview, Dec. 30, 1985; Hummel, interview, May 14, 1984.

45. Parke-Bernet Galleries, *Furniture and Decorations: Estate of the Late Louis Rorimer, April 25, 26, and 27, 1940* (New York: Parke-Bernet, 1940).

46. "19,900 Paid at Art Sale," *New York Times,* April 28, 1940, p. 36, col. 2.

47. Karen Davies, "American Decorative Arts of the Late 1920's," *Antiques,* Dec. 1983, p. 1212; Dushkin, interview, Aug. 8, 1985.

48. Dushkin, interview, Aug. 8, 1985.

49. Parke-Bernet, *Furniture and Decorations*, "Memoir"; Parke-Bernet, *Furniture and Decorations*, pp. 66 and 104; *Cleveland News*, Apr. 13, 1940 (clipping on file at the Cleveland Public Library).

50. Lot number 365 was described in the catalog as, "Claret ground decorated with gold festoons and cartouches reserved in white and printed with clusters of flowers en camaieu in gold, enhanced with gilded highlights. Length 27 rolls; width 18 inches."

51. Frank Copley and W. H. Glover, "The Birge Story," *Niagara Frontier* (Buffalo: Buffalo and Erie County Historical Society, Spring 1959), pp. 2 and 8.

52. "Rorimer-Brooks, Itemization of Purchases Since 1935," Dr. R. W. Scott.

53. French, "Head and Shoulders," p. 13.

CHAPTER 4. COMMERCIAL WORK

1. For a partial list of clients, see appendix A.

2. Floyd Miller, *Statler* (New York: Statler Foundation, 1968), pp. 108–9.

3. William Ganson Rose, *Cleveland: The Making of a City* (Cleveland: World, 1950), p. 614. In 1846 the parcel had been sold for $100 an acre ("Prepare the Way for Euclid-Av Hotel," *Cleveland Plain Dealer*, Oct. 26, 1910, p. 1; Miller, *Statler*, p. 110).

4. Miller, *Statler*, p. 112.

5. Ibid., p. 114; Rose, *Cleveland*, p. 712; Miller, *Statler*, p. 119.

6. Miller, *Statler*, p. 133.

7. May N. Stone, "Hotel Pennsylvania: Strictly First-Class Accommodations at Affordable Rates" (master's thesis, Columbia University, 1988), pp. 67–70.

8. Miller, *Statler*, p. 113; evidence for this can be found in numerous entries of the "Shop Detail Book" from 1929 to 1938; untitled clipping from a Cleveland newspaper stamped June 17, 1928 (on file at Cleveland Public Library).

9. "Splendid New Public Dining Rooms Opened in Statler Hotels of Cleveland and Detroit," *The Western Hotel and Restaurant Reporter* 62, no. 2 (Feb. 1938): 9, 10, and 22.

10. Ibid., p. 8.

11. Alice Statler from the Hotel Pennsylvania in New York to Rorimer in Cleveland, Nov. 15, 1938, and on Nov. 25, 1938.

12. Alice Statler to Rorimer, Aug. 3, 1939; "Goes Abroad to Buy Art Objects for Statler Hotel," *Boston Eve Transcript*, March 24, 1926, unpaginated.

13. Miller, *Statler*, p. 113.

14. J. O. Dahl and M. Crete, "Greenbrier—A History of Hospitality, *Hotel World Pictorial*, April 1931, p. 1.

15. Ibid., pp. 1 and 8; Robert S. Conte, Greenbrier Historian, letter to the author, April 26, 1985.

16. Dahl and Crete, "Greenbrier," illustrations on pp. 3–8; Conte to author, April 26, 1985; Robert S. Conte, *The History of the Greenbrier: America's Resort* (Charleston, W. Va.: Pictorial Histories, 1989).

17. Ian S. Haberman, *The Van Sweringens of Cleveland: The Biography of an Empire* (Cleveland: WRHS, 1979), p. 152; Conte to author, April 26, 1985.

18. The Phyfe dining set bore marks stamped on the bottom of the chair seats that were not a Rorimer-Brooks label because the chairs were designed at Rorimer-Brooks and probably manufactured elsewhere. (Probala, telephone interview, Sept. 24, 1986.)

19. "The Carter Imprint on the White House," *U.S. News and World Report* 86, no. 12 (March 26, 1979): 66.

20. Rose, *Cleveland*, p. 860; Probala, interview, May 25, 1985.

21. Haberman, *The Van Sweringens*, p. 152; oversized photographs can be seen at the WRHS Library under Ohio residences: Hunting Valley, Daisy Hill, but are otherwise uncataloged.

22. Probala, telephone interviews, Sept. 24, 1986 and Dec. 26, 1989; Robert Bordner, "Louis Rorimer Designs Modern Furniture," unpaginated article, CMA file; Michele Lesie, "At Silver Grille, Memories, Misgivings," *Cleveland Plain Dealer*, Dec. 23, 1989, pp. A–10 and A–12; neither

General Fireproofing nor Dunbar in Indiana have records dating back far enough to supply information about the furniture.

23. Probala, telephone interview, Sept. 24, 1986.

24. "J. T. Meals, Head of Taylor Chair," *Cleveland Plain Dealer*, June 4, 1986, obituary page.

25. Taylor Chair Company, *The Taylor Chair Company: Seven Generations Since 1816* (Bedford, Ohio: Taylor Chair, 1982), p. 14. Fitch was a direct descendent of the famous Rev. James Fitch, who came to this country in 1638 at the age of 16, and who is variously described as "one of the founders of Saybrook and Norwich, Conn., founder of Beagnon, Conn., and Envoy Extraordinary of the Colonists to the Indian Chiefs during King Phillip's War." His son, James Fitch, founded Yale College.

26. Ibid., pp. 19 and 20. He was six generations removed from John Taylor of Haverill, England, who "bound himself out" to pay for his passage to the New World with Gov. John Winthrop in 1630.

27. Ibid., p. 37.

28. "Taylor-Horrocks Executive Suites, Authentic Period Designs," *Catalogue No. 122 Special Recorded Edition* book no. 406 (Bedford, Ohio: Taylor Chair [1930]); Taylor Chair, *Taylor Chair*, pp. 41 and 42. As early as 1914 the Taylor Chair Company titled a page in its record book "Rorheimer-Brooks" (this was earlier than 1917 when the name was changed to Rorimer). Entries include dates from 1915 to 1924 and appear to have been purchases made by Rorimer-Brooks.

29. Taylor Chair saved xerox copies of the drawings and Andrew Probala saved a portfolio of the originals. Many of these drawings are in the WRHS Library oversize collection (accessions 83–90 and 83–96).

30. "Taylor-Horrocks Executive Suites."

31. "American Modern Art" *Good Furniture Magazine* 27, no. 4 (Oct. 1926): 173; Matson, "Louis Rorimer—Businessman of Art."

32. Greif, *Depression Modern*, pp. 28 and 42.

33. Similarly styled bedroom pieces by designer Eugene Schoen are illustrated in R. L. Leonard and C. A. Glassgold, eds., *Annual of American Design 1931* (New York: Ives Washburn, 1930), p. 37. The *Annual* exemplified state-of-the-art modern American design in 1930.

34. Tom Dewey II, *Art Nouveau, Art Deco, and Modernism: A Guide to the Styles 1890–1940* (Jackson, Miss.: Mississippi Museum of Art, 1983), plate 66, p. 43.

35. "American Modernist Furniture," *Good Furniture Magazine* 29, no. 3 (Sept. 1927): 119–21.

36. Henry-Russell Hitchcock, Jr., "Some American Interiors in the Modern Style," *Architectural Record*, Sept. 1928, p. 236.

37. Rosenthal and Ratzka, *The Story of Modern Applied Art*, pp. 175–76.

38. Sanford, "Decorating in Art Moderne," p. 241.

39. Nellie C. Sanford, "An Architect-Designer of Modern Furniture," *Good Furniture Magazine* 30, no. 3 (March 1928): 118.

40. See Karen Davies, *At Home in Manhattan: Modern Decorative Arts, 1925 to the Depression* (New Haven, Conn.: Yale Univ. Art Gallery, 1983), p. 26.

41. Probala, interviews, May 29, 1984 and Dec. 26, 1989; William Van Alen, "The Structure and Metal Work of the Chrysler Building," *The Architectural Forum* 53, no. 4 (Oct. 1930): 494 and 497.

42. Calvin Tomkins, "The Cloisters . . . The Cloisters . . . The Cloisters," *Metropolitan Museum of Art Bulletin*, March 1970, p. 316.

43. James Rorimer, letter to his father, Sept. 28, 1925, in Rorimer Archives; James J. Rorimer, *The Metropolitan Museum of Art: The Cloisters* (New York, 1939), preface.

44. Tomkins, "The Cloisters," p. 320.

CHAPTER 5. RESIDENTIAL

1. "English and Early American Homes in Favor," *Good Furniture Magazine* 27, no. 2 (Aug. 1926): 74.

2. Lewis Mumford, "American Taste," *Harpers Monthly* 155 (Oct. 1927): 569–77; David Hanks and Jennifer Toher, "1900–1915: Tradition and Reform," in Whitney Museum of Art, *High Style: Twentieth Century American Design* (New York: Whitney Museum, 1986), p. 3.

3. Robbins, "Louis Rorimer," p. 35.

4. See for example, David Gebhard, "1915–1930 Traditionalism and Design: Old Models for the New," in Whitney Museum of Art, *High Style;* Dianne Pilgrim, "Decorative Art: The Domestic Environment," in Brooklyn Museum, *The American Renaissance 1876–1917* (Brooklyn: Brooklyn Museum, 1979); Kenneth Ames, "Introduction," in Alan Axelrod, ed., *The Colonial Revival in America* (New York: Norton, 1985); Celia Betsky, "Inside the Past: The Interior and the Colonial Revival in American Art and Literature 1860–1914," in Axelrod, *Colonial Revival in America.*

5. Rorimer was often quoted on his dislike of machinery, and he also blamed machines for driving out handcrafted and individually designed furniture with their mass imitations. Robert Bordner, "Battles for Beauty in Furniture Art," *Cleveland Press*, July 4, 1929, p. 18; Bordner, "Louis Rorimer Designs Modern Furniture," p. 5.

6. See for example, C. H. Baer, *Farbige Raumkunst*, vol. 2 (Stuttgart: Julius Hoffman, 1914), p. 15 by Alfred Schulze, p. 69 by Tom Merry, and p. 77 by Robert Hammes; Alexander Koch, *Farbige Wohnräume der Neuzeit* (Darmstadt: Alexander Koch, 1926), pp. 1 and 2 by Franz Kuhn, p. 6 by Alfred Wenzel, and p. 59 by Hugo Gorge.

7. Joseph T. Butler, *Field Guide to American Antique Furniture* (New York: Facts on File, 1985), p. 18; Oscar Fitzgerald, *Three Centuries of American Furniture* (Englewood Cliffs, N.J.: Prentice-Hall, 1982), p. 13.

8. Candace Wheeler, *Principles of Home Decoration* (Garden City, N.Y.: Doubleday, Page, 1903); William A. Vollmer, ed., *A Book of Distinctive Interiors* (New York: McBride, Nast, 1912); Reginald Townsend, *The Book of Building and Interior Decoration* (Garden City, N.Y.: Doubleday, Page, 1923); Bernard Jakway, *The Principles of Interior Decoration* (New York: Macmillan, 1923); Edward Stratton Holloway, *The Practical Book of Learning Decoration and Furniture* (Philadelphia: J. P. Lippincott, 1926); Lurelle Guild, *Designed for Living: The Blue Book of Interior Decoration* (Scranton, Penn.: Scranton Lace, 1936).

9. Advocates of historic styles included William A. Vollmer, Reginald Townsend, Wallace Nutting, and Edward Stratton Holloway. Modernists included members of the American Union of Decorative Artists and Craftsmen (AUDAC), especially Paul Frankl who also published books on modern design. Advocates of both historic and modern styles included Candace Wheeler, Bernard Jakway, and Lurelle Guild.

10. Wheeler, *Principles of Home Decoration*, p. 163, 169, and 181.

11. Townsend, *The Book of Building and Interior Decoration*, foreword.

12. Jakway, *The Principles of Interior Decoration*, pp. 278 and 279.

13. Ibid., p. 280.

14. Ibid., p. 274.

15. Holloway, *The Practical Book of Learning Decoration and Furniture*, p. 17.

16. Ibid., p. 17.

17. Guild, *Designed for Living*, pp. 8–9.

18. Ibid., p. 29.

19. Quoted in William L. Dulaney, "Wallace Nutting: Collector and Entrepreneur," in Ian Quimby, ed., *American Furniture and Its Makers: Winterthur Portfolio* 13 (Chicago: Univ. of Chicago Press, 1979), p. 60.

20. In a letter from Rorimer to Grace Ellis (April 18, 1939, in Rorimer Archives), Rorimer stated that "We do most of our buying abroad." Nutting's books were included in the Rorimer-Brooks 1939 "Inventory Book" (Rorimer Archives), as were many other books on furniture history.

21. See for example, Alastair Duncan, *Art Nouveau Furniture* (New York: Clarkson N. Potter, 1982), plate 28, "chaise orchides" circa 1902 by Louis Majorelle.

22. Also about 1912, Rorimer designed and made furniture for the Magnolia Drive home of his brother-in-law, Abe Stearn, founder of Stearn Brothers Department Store in Cleveland. Following the death of Stearn's son Louis, the set was moved to Bigsbluff.

23. Triggs, *History of the Arts and Crafts Movement*, pp. 35–37; Mario Amaya, *Art Nouveau* (London: Studio Vista, 1966), p. 11; Duncan, *Art Nouveau Furniture*, plates 126 and 157, and p. 171.

24. See for example, Gerald Larner and Celia Larner, *The Glasgow Style* (New York: Taplinger, 1979), plates 12, 55, 70, 143, 144, 182, and 183.

25. Larner and Larner, *Glasgow Style*, plates 159 and 22; Anscombe and Gere, *Arts and Crafts in Britain and America*, plates 310 and 142.

26. John Fleming and Hugh Honour, *Dictionary of the Decorative Arts* (London: Allen Lane, 1977; reprint, New York: Harper and Row, 1986), pp. 263–64; Edward Lucie-Smith, *Furniture: A Concise History* (New York: Oxford Univ. Press, 1979), pp. 117–19; Carol L. Bohdan, "Egyptian-Inspired Furniture 1800–1922," *Art and Antiques* 3, no. 6 (Nov.–Dec. 1980): 65 and 69.

27. Robert Bishop and Patricia Coblentz, *American Decorative Arts: 360 Years of Creative Design* (New York: Harry Abrams, 1982), pp. 44–49 and 267; Martin Battersby, *The Decorative Twenties* (New York: Walker, 1969), p. 142; Philip Johnson, who was never known for his admiration of interior designers, was recently asked what he thought about Rorimer. He replied, "I now admire him. I admire his versatility and fine craftsmanship." Mrs. John Dempsey to the author, n.d.

28. See for example, the Cyrus Clark Ford house featured in "Height Style," a brochure published for the Heights Heritage Tour (Cleveland, 1985); Shirley Fernberg, "Stately Heights Home has Space, Privacy," *Habitat* (Dec. 6–12, 1985), p. 1.

29. Rorimer was well known for his love of entertaining (Frary, "Louis Rorimer 1872–1939," p. 3.

30. Helen Thackrey, "A House and Garden in the Woods," *Your Garden* 3, no. 6 (Oct. 1929): 15.

31. Leo Marx, *The Machine in the Garden: Technology and the Pastoral Ideal in America* (New York: Oxford Univ. Press, 1964), p. 23.

32. Koch, *Farbige Wohnräume der Neuzeit*, various illustrations, such as p. 1 by Wiener Werkstätte designer Franz Kuhn, p. 6 by Alfred Wenzel, p. 18 by Theodore Pfeiffer, and p. 32 by Reinhold and Margarete Stotz. Rorimer had regularly visited New York, where in 1922 Joseph Urban had opened a showroom introducing examples of work by the foremost Wiener Werkstätte artists (Galerie St. Etienne, *Wiener Werkstaette* [New York: Galerie St. Etienne, 1966], p. 1).

33. Motifs resemble work by noted Wiener Werkstätte designers Dagobert Peche and Karl Czeschka (Schweiger, *Wiener Werkstaette*, bottom p. 113 and top p. 212).

34. Thackrey, "House and Garden," p. 39.

35. Advertisement, *Your Garden* 4, no. 4 (Aug. 1930), inside front cover; Cleveland Orchestra special concert program (Feb. 5–7, 1931) for the dedication of Severence Hall.

36. "American Modernist Furniture," pp. 119–21.

37. Davies, *At Home in Manhattan*, pp. 20, 21, 23, and 26.

38. See for example, *Good Furniture Magazine*, Oct. 1926; March, Sept., Oct., and Nov. 1927; July, Sept., and Nov. 1928; Jan. 1929.

39. "Art Moderne Furniture Design in America," *Good Furniture Magazine*, Oct. 1927, p. 179.

40. W. Frank Purdy, "The Taste of the American People," *Arts and Decoration*, Nov. 1920, p. 38.

41. See for example, Dewey, *Art Nouveau, Art Deco, and Modernism*, p. 43; Leonard and Glassgold, *Annual of American Design 1931*, p. 36; "American Modernist Furniture," p. 120.

42. Paul Frankl, *Form and Re-Form* (New York: Harper and Brothers, 1930), pp. 91, 93, and 99.

43. Bordner, "Louis Rorimer Designs Modern Furniture," p. 5.

44. Rosenthal and Ratzka, *The Story of Modern Applied Art*, pp. 185 and 192.

45. Cara Greenberg, *Mid-Century Modern* (New York: Harmony Books, 1984), p. 14.

46. Bordner, "Louis Rorimer Designs Modern Furniture," p. 5.

47. John Loring, "American Deco," *Connoisseur*, Jan. 1979, p. 51; Greenberg, *Mid-Century Modern*, p. 17.

48. Dorothy Raley, ed., *A Century of Progress: Homes and Furnishings* (Chicago: M. A. Ring, 1934), see for example pp. 20, 22, 83, and 85; for examples of Thirties Modern, pp. 31, 57, 86, 105, and 114; for examples of radical modern, pp. 37, 39, 41, and 73.

49. Greenberg, *Mid-Century Modern*, p. 21.

50. Rosemarie Haag Bletter, "1930–1945 The World of Tomorrow: The Future with a Past," in Whitney Museum of Art, *High Style*, p. 122.

51. Esther McCoy, "1945–1960 The Rationalist Period," in Whitney Museum of Art, *High Style*, p. 142.

52. Frary, "Louis Rorimer 1872–1939," p. 4.

BIBLIOGRAPHY

PRIMARY SOURCES

Of the primary sources consulted, personal interviews were particularly important, because the information they contained could not have been found elsewhere. Two former employees of Louis Rorimer, Andrew E. Probala and Phillip T. Hummel, and his daughter Louise were most informative.

Manuscript records of the Rorimer-Brooks Studios were destroyed in 1957. However, a collection of material specifically about Rorimer and his company was discovered in 1986. These letters, newspaper clippings, magazine articles, company documents, photographs, and original drawings were collected by Rorimer's son James and are now in the possession of James's widow, Katherine Rorimer. It is anticipated that these Rorimer Archives will be deposited at either the Western Reserve Historical Society (WRHS) in Cleveland, Ohio, or the Metropolitan Museum of Art in New York.

Bellfaire staff members. Telephone interview. June 1, 1985.

Campen, Richard. "Louis Rorimer 1872–1939." Ms. (typescript) Aug. 1964. Copy given to author by Louis Rorimer II.

Carome, Ed (son of furniture finisher Michele Carome). Telephone interview. June 5, 1985.

Cincinnati Historical Society. Collection of newspaper clippings. Copies of obituaries for Rorimer and the Joseph family members were given to the author by Derek Ostergard.

Cleveland Arts Club. "Cleveland Arts Club, Cleveland, Ohio, Record Book 1913–1917." Manuscript collection, WRHS Library, Cleveland.

Cleveland Section, National Council of Jewish Women Records. "Autumn Social Minutes, October 29, 1903." Container 2, folder 3. WRHS Library, Cleveland.

Cleveland Institute of Art. "Scrapbook." Microfilmed collection of newspaper articles concerning faculty. CIA Library, Cleveland.

————. List of past officers in library manuscript collection.

Cleveland Museum of Art. Copies of letters from museum staff to Rorimer and Rorimer-Brooks. Office of CMA Director, Cleveland.

————. Folder containing newspaper clippings and pamphlets. Artist File Collection, CMA Library, Cleveland.

Cleveland Orchestra. Archives. Severence Hall, Cleveland.

Cleveland Public Library. Folder containing clippings from Cleveland newspapers.

Dushkin, Louise Rorimer. Personal interviews. May 29, 1985 and Aug. 8, 1985.

Fillous, Bob. Telephone interview. May 30, 1985.

Frary, Ihna Thayer. "Louis Rorimer 1872–1939." Eulogy delivered on Dec. 1939 at the Paul Feiss home, Cleveland Heights. Copy to be deposited at WRHS, Cleveland.

———. "Scrapbook." Manuscript 3144, "Ihna Thayer Frary 1873–1965." WRHS Library, Cleveland.

Geismer, Alan. Personal interview. Feb. 9, 1985.

Green, William B. Drawings of designs for Taylor Chair. [c. 1930.] Accessions 83–90 and 83–96, WRHS Library, Cleveland.

———. Renderings of designs for Taylor Chair. [c. 1930.] Property of Andrew Probala.

Hummel, Phillip T. Personal interview. May 14, 1984.

———. Telephone interview. Dec. 30, 1985.

Probala, Andrew E. Personal interviews. May 29, 1984, May 25, 1985, May 29, 1985, June 25, 1985.

———. Telephone interviews on Sept. 24, 1986 and Dec. 26, 1989.

Rohrheimer, Bella. Letters to Katherine Bang-Kohn, Louis Rorimer, and others. 1939–40. WRHS Library, Cleveland.

Rohrheimer, Louis. Student Portfolio. Munich Kunstgewerbeschule, 1891. Property of Louise Rorimer Dushkin.

Rorimer Archives. Collection of handwritten and printed material from 1891 to 1940 by or about Rorimer. Property of Mrs. James Rorimer.

Rorimer, Louis. "Art in Relation to the Industries." Convention of the American Federation of Arts, May 15, 1925. Copy to be deposited at WRHS, Cleveland.

———. "Shop Detail Book." [1929–38.] Property of Andrew Probala. Copy to be deposited at WRHS Library, Cleveland.

Rorimer, Mrs. James (Katherine). Personal interviews. May 29, 1985, May 28, 1986, June 6, 1986, June 14, 1986, Dec. 25, 1989.

Rorimer-Brooks. "Itemization of Purchases Since 1935" for Dr. R. W. Scott. Typescript, in author's possession.

Rowfant Club. "A Register of its Records (1891–1973)." Manuscript processed by Catherine Stover in 1973. Manuscript collection, WRHS Library, Cleveland.

Schreckengost, Viktor. Personal interview. May 6, 1985.

Tefereth Israel Congregation. "Minutes." 1901. The Temple Library, Cleveland.

Van Sweringen, Daisy Hill, Hunting Valley, Ohio. Photographs. Oversize collection, WRHS Library, Cleveland.

SECONDARY SOURCES

Amaya, Mario. *Art Nouveau.* London: Studio Vista, 1966.

American Federation of Arts. *American Art Annual: 1932*, vol. 29. Washington, D.C.: American Federation of Arts, 1933.

———. *American Art Annual: 1934*, vol. 30. Washington, D.C.: American Federation of Arts, 1935.

"American Modern Art." *Good Furniture Magazine* 27, no. 4 (Oct. 1926): 172–74.

"American Modernist Furniture." *Good Furniture Magazine* 29, no. 3 (Sept. 1927): 119–21.

American Society of Interior Designers. *Annual Report 1980.* New York: ASID, 1981.

American Union of Decorative Artists and Craftsmen. *AUDAC Exhibition.* New York: Brooklyn Museum, 1931.

Ames, Kenneth. "Introduction." In *The Colonial Revival in America. See* Axelrod, 1985.

Anscombe, Isabelle, and Charlotte Gere. *Arts and Crafts in Britain and America.* London: Academy, 1978.

Art and Antiques, ed. *Nineteenth Century Furniture: Innovation, Revival, and Reform.* New York: Billboard, 1982.

"Art Moderne at the Midsummer Markets." *Good Furniture Magazine,* Sept. 1928, pp. 118–26.

"Art Moderne for a Conservative Clientele." *Good Furniture Magazine,* Sept. 1928, pp. 131–33.

"Art Moderne Furniture Design in America." *Good Furniture Magazine,* Oct. 1927, pp. 179–82.

Aslin, Elizabeth. *The Aesthetic Movement: Prelude to Art Nouveau.* London: Elek, 1969. Reprint. New York: Excalibur, 1981.

"At Stag Party in Play House." *Cleveland Press,* June 5, 1937.

"AUDAC Exhibition, The." *Brooklyn Museum Quarterly* 18 (July 1931): 93–97.

Axelrod, Alan, ed. *The Colonial Revival in America.* New York: Norton, 1985.

Baer, C. H. *Farbige Raumkunst.* Stuttgart: Julius Hoffman, 1914.

Bassham, Ben, ed. *The Memories of an American Impressionist: Abel G. Warshawsky.* Kent, Ohio: Kent State Univ. Press, 1980.

Bates, Elizabeth Bidwell, and Jonathan L. Fairbanks. *American Furniture 1620 to the Present.* New York: Richard Marek, 1981.

Battersby, Martin. *The Decorative Twenties.* New York: Walker, 1969.

――――. *The Decorative Thirties.* New York: Walker, 1971.

Beard, Miriam. "Business Cultivates the Arts." *New York Times Magazine,* Jan. 31, 1926.

Bernays, Edward L. *Biography of an Idea: Memoirs of Public Relations Consul Edward L. Bernays.* New York: Simon and Schuster, 1965.

Betsky, Celia. "Inside the Past: The Interior and the Colonial Revival in American Art and Literature 1860–1914." In *The Colonial Revival in America. See* Axelrod, 1985.

Bing and Haas, eds. *The Temple 1850–1950.* Cleveland: The Temple.

Bing, Samuel. *Artistic America, Tiffany Glass, and Art Nouveau.* Cambridge: MIT Press, 1970.

Bishop, Robert. *The American Chair: Three Centuries of Style.* New York: Dutton, 1972. Reprint. New York: Bonanza, 1983.

Bishop Robert, and Patricia Coblentz. *American Decorative Arts: 360 Years of Creative Design.* New York: Harry Abrams, 1982.

Bletter, Rosemarie Haag. "1930–1945 The World of Tomorrow: The Future with a Past." In *High Style. See* Whitney Museum of Art, 1986.

Bohdan, Carol L. "Egyptian-Inspired Furniture 1800–1922." *Art and Antiques* 3, no. 6 (Nov.–Dec. 1980): 64–71.

Book of Clevelanders, The: A Biographical Dictionary of Living Men of the City of Cleveland. Cleveland: Burrows Bros., 1914.

Bordner, Robert. "Battles for Beauty in Furniture Art." *Cleveland Press,* July 4, 1929, p. 18.

――――. "Louis Rorimer Designs Modern Furniture." *Cleveland Plain Dealer,* Nov. 7, 1931, p. 5.

Brandt, Frederick. *Late 19th and Early 20th Century Decorative Arts.* Richmond, Va.: Virginia Museum of Fine Arts, 1985.

Brooklyn Museum. *The American Renaissance 1876–1917*. Brooklyn: Brooklyn Museum, 1979.

Brooks, Charles S. "The Cleveland Play House." *Theatre Arts Monthly*, Aug. 1926, pp. 516–22.

Brooks Household Art Company. *The House Beautiful*. Cleveland: Brooks Household Art Company [1900].

Brown, Erica. *Sixty Years of Interior Design: The World of McMillen*. New York: Viking, 1982.

Bush, Donald. *The Streamlined Decade*. New York: Braziller, 1975.

Butler, Joseph T. *Field Guide to American Antique Furniture*. New York: Facts on File, 1985.

Carroll, Mitchel, et al. "Activities of the Arts Club of Washington." *Art and Archaeology*, Aug. 1921, pp. 7–12.

"Carter Imprint on the White House, The." *U.S. News and World Report* 86, no. 12 (March 26, 1979): 66.

Century Furniture Company. *Furniture as Interpreted by the Century Furniture Company*. Grand Rapids: Century Furniture, 1931.

Clark, Edna Maria. *Ohio Art and Artists*. Richmond: Garrett and Massie, 1932. Reprint. Detroit: Gale Research, 1975.

Clark, Robert Judson, ed. *The Arts and Crafts Movement in America 1876–1916*. Princeton, N.J.: Princeton Univ. Press, 1972.

Cleveland. Chicago: Lewis, 1918.

Cleveland Amusement Gazette. Dec. 21, 1895.

Cleveland Architectural Club. *Exhibition Catalogues*. Cleveland, 1896, 1897, 1900, 1901, and 1909.

Cleveland Chamber of Commerce. *Medals Awarded for Merit in Building 1917*. Cleveland: Chamber of Commerce, 1917.

Cleveland City Directory. Cleveland, 1853–92 and 1904–17.

"Cleveland Convention, The." *American Magazine of Art*. July 1925, p. 348.

Cleveland Manual Training School. Cleveland, June 1899.

Cleveland Museum of Art. *Bulletin of the Cleveland Museum of Art*. May–June 1919–28. Cleveland: CMA.

Cleveland Society of Artists. *Silhouette*. Cleveland, 1939. On file in Cleveland Museum of Art Library "artist files."

Cleveland Topics. Portrait of Rorimer. Jan. 20, 1917.

Cohen, Lizabeth. "Embellishing a Life of Labor: An Interpretation of the Material Culture of American Working Class Homes 1885–1915." *Jr. American Culture* 3 (Winter 1980): 752–75.

Conte, Robert S. *The History of the Greenbrier: America's Resort*. Charleston, W. Va.: Pictorial Histories, 1989.

Copley, Frank, and W. H. Glover. "The Birge Story." *Niagara Frontier*, Spring 1959, pp. 1–18. Buffalo: Buffalo and Erie County Historical Society.

Dahl, J. O., and M. Crete. "Greenbrier—A History of Hospitality." *Hotel World Pictorial*, April 1931, pp. 1–15.

Davidson, Marshall B., ed. *Three Centuries of American Antiques*. New York: Bonanza, 1979.

Davidson, Marshall B., and Elizabeth Stillinger. *The American Wing at the Metropolitan Museum of Art*. New York: Alfred A. Knopf, 1985.

Davies, Karen. "American Decorative Arts of the Late 1920's." *Antiques*, Dec. 1983, pp. 1212–17.

———. *At Home in Manhattan: Modern Decorative Arts 1925 to the Depression.* New Haven: Yale Univ. Art Gallery, 1983.

"Decorative Artists Form Union." *Architectural Record,* Aug. 1928, p. 164.

Dewey, Tom, II. *Art Nouveau, Art Deco, and Modernism: A Guide to the Styles 1890–1940.* Jackson, Miss.: Mississippi Museum of Art, 1983.

Dulaney, William L. "Wallace Nutting: Collector and Entrepreneur." In Ian Quimby, ed., *American Furniture and Its Makers: Winterthur Portfolio 13:* 47–60. Chicago: Univ. of Chicago Press, 1979.

Duncan, Alastair. *Art Nouveau Furniture.* New York: Clarkson N. Potter, 1982.

———. *Art Deco Furniture.* New York: Holt, Rinehart and Winston, 1984.

"Dwellings of the Middle West." *Architectural Record,* Oct. 1904, p. 377.

"English and Early American Homes in Favor." *Good Furniture Magazine* 27, no. 2 (August 1926): 73–75.

"Exhibition of the Cleveland Architectural Club." *Ohio Architect and Builder* 14 (Nov. 1909): 53–55.

"Expects New Trend in Decorative Arts." *New York Times,* Aug. 16, 1925, p. 26, col. 1.

Faude, Wilson H. "Associated Artists and the American Renaissance in the Decorative Arts." In Ian Quimby, ed., *Winterthur Portfolio 10.* Charlottesville, Va.: University Press of Virginia, 1975.

Fernberg, Shirley. "Stately Heights Home Has Space, Privacy." *Habitat,* Dec. 6–12, 1985, p. 1.

Fisher, Steven. "Ihna Thayer Frary: Register of His Papers 1895–1963 in the Western Reserve Historical Society." WRHS Library, Cleveland, 1976.

Fitzgerald, Oscar. *Three Centuries of American Furniture.* Englewood Cliffs, N.J.: Prentice-Hall, 1982.

"Five Institutions are Willed $6,659." *Cleveland Plain Dealer,* Aug. 25, 1954.

Fleming, John and Hugh Honour. *Dictionary of the Decorative Arts.* London: Allen Lane, 1977. Reprint. New York: Harper and Row, 1986.

Frangiamore, Ray. *A Thing of Beauty: Art Nouveau, Art Deco, Arts and Crafts Movement, and Aesthetic Movement Objects in Atlanta Collections.* Atlanta: High Museum of Art, 1980.

Frankl, Paul. *New Dimensions.* New York: Brewer and Warren, 1928.

———. *Form and Re-Form.* New York: Harper and Bros., 1930.

———. "The Home of Yesterday, Today and Tomorrow." In *Annual of American Design 1931. See* Leonard and Glassgold, 1930.

"French Art Moderne Exposition in New York." *Good Furniture Magazine,* Sept. 1928, pp. 119–22.

French, Winsor. "Head and Shoulders: Impresario of the Arts." *Parade,* Sept. 22, 1932, pp. 12, 13, and 28.

Galerie, St. Etienne. *Wiener Werkstaette.* New York: Galerie St. Etienne, 1966.

Garner, Philippe. *The Encyclopedia of Decorative Arts 1890–1940.* New York: Van Nostrand Reinhold, 1978.

Gartner, Lloyd P. *History of the Jews in Cleveland.* Cleveland: WRHS and Jewish Theological Seminary, 1978.

Gebhard, David. "1915–1930 Traditionalism and Design: Old Models for the New." In *High Style. See* Whitney Museum of Art, 1986.

Gilman, Roger. "The Paris Exposition: A Glimpse into the Future." *Art Bulletin,* Sept. 1925, pp. 33–42.

"Goes Abroad to Buy Art Objects for Statler Hotel." *Boston Eve Transcript,* March 24, 1926.

Greenberg, Cara. *Mid-Century Modern.* New York: Harmony Books, 1984.

Greif, Martin. *Depression Modern: The Thirties Style in America.* New York: Universe Books, 1975.

Guild, Lurelle. *Designed for Living: The Blue Book of Interior Decoration.* Scranton, Penn.: Scranton Lace, 1936.

Haberman, Ian S. *The Van Sweringens of Cleveland: The Biography of an Empire.* Cleveland: WRHS, 1979.

Hanks, David, and Jennifer Toher. "1900–1915: Tradition and Reform." In *High Style. See* Whitney Museum of Art, 1986.

"Height Style." Cleveland: Heights Heritage Tour, 1985.

Hepplewhite, George. *The Cabinet-Maker and Upholsterer's Guide.* 3rd ed. London: I. and J. Taylor, 1794. Reprint. New York: Dover, 1969.

Hitchcock, Henry-Russell, Jr. "Some American Interiors in the Modern Style." *Architectural Record,* Sept. 1928, pp. 235–42.

Holloway, Edward Stratton. *The Practical Book of Learning Decoration and Furniture.* Philadelphia: J. P. Lippincott, 1926.

Homer, William Innes. *Robert Henri and His Circle.* Ithaca, N.Y.: Cornell Univ. Press, 1969.

"Honored by Decorators." *Cleveland Plain Dealer,* July 1, 1934.

"In Memoriam—Louis Rorimer." *Bulletin of the Cleveland Museum of Art,* Feb. 1940, p. 16.

"Interior Decorators Organize." *Cleveland Bystander,* Nov. 14, 1931, p. 19.

Jakway, Bernard. *The Principles of Interior Decoration.* New York: MacMillan, 1923.

Kaplan, Wendy. *The Art That Is Life: The Arts and Crafts Movement in America, 1875–1920.* Boston: Little, Brown, 1987.

Kelly, Grace. "Art Museum Given Rorimer Memorial." *Cleveland Plain Dealer,* April 26, 1946.

Klein, Dan. "The Chrysler Building." *The American Connoisseur,* April 1974, pp. 294–301.

Koch, Alexander. *Farbige Wohnräume der Neuzeit.* Darmstadt: Alexander Koch, 1926.

Koch, Robert. *Louis C. Tiffany: Rebel in Glass.* Updated 3d ed. New York: Crown, 1982.

Larner, Gerald, and Celia Larner. *The Glasgow Style.* New York: Taplinger, 1979.

Learoyd, Stan. *A Guide to English Antique Furniture Construction and Decoration 1500–1910.* New York: Van Nostrand Reinhold, 1981.

Lears, Jackson. *No Place of Grace: Antimodernism and the Transformation of American Culture 1880–1920.* New York: Pantheon, 1981.

Leonard, R. L. and C. A. Glassgold, eds. *Annual of American Design 1931.* New York: Ives Washburn, 1930.

Lesie, Michele. "At Silver Grille, Memories, Misgivings." *Cleveland Plain Dealer,* Dec. 23, 1989, A-10 and A-12.

Loring, John. "American Deco." *Connoisseur,* Jan. 1979, pp. 49–53.

"Louis Rorimer." *Cincinnati Enquirer,* Dec. 2, 1939.

"Louis Rorimer Dies; Artist and Decorator." *Cleveland News,* Nov. 30, 1939.

"Louis Rorimer is Dead at 67." *Cleveland Press,* Nov. 30, 1939.

"Louis Rorimer Merits Praise in Art Labors." *Suburban News and Herald,* Feb. 23, 1934.

"Louis Rorimer, 67, Artist, Decorator." *New York Times,* Dec. 1, 1939.

Lucie-Smith, Edward. *Furniture: A Concise History.* New York: Oxford Univ. Press, 1979.

McConnell, Frederic. "The Cleveland Playhouse." *Architectural Record* 62 (Aug. 1927): 81–94.

McCoy, Esther. "1945–1960 The Rationalist Period." In *High Style*. *See* Whitney Museum of Art, 1986.

McGregor, Donald. "AUDAC in Brooklyn." *Good Furniture and Decoration*, June 1931, pp. 322–25.

Madigan, Mary Jean, and Susan Colgan, eds. *Early American Furniture From Settlement to City*. New York: Billboard, 1983.

Marx, Leo. *The Machine in the Garden: Technology and the Pastoral Ideal in America*. New York: Oxford Univ. Press, 1964.

Masina, Lara-Vinca. *Art Nouveau*. Secaucus, N.J.: Chartwell, 1984.

Matson, Carlton. "Louis Rorimer—Businessman of Art." *Cleveland Press*, Nov. 10, 1932.

"J. T. Meals, Head of Taylor Chair." *Cleveland Plain Dealer*, June 4, 1986.

Meikle, Jeffrey L. *Twentieth Century Limited: Industrial Design in America 1925–1939*. Philadelphia: Temple Univ. Press, 1979.

"Memorial Today to Honor Rorimer." *Cleveland Plain Dealer*, Dec. 1, 1939.

Menten, Theodore. *The Art Deco Style*. New York: Dover, 1972.

Miller, Floyd. *Statler*. New York: Statler Foundation, 1968.

"Mr. Rorheimer's Decorative Department." *Cleveland Topics*, Jan. 20, 1917, p. 26.

"Mr. Rorimer's Appointment." *Cleveland Topics*, May 23, 1925, p. 24.

"Modern Decorative Arts from Paris at the Metropolitan Museum of Art." *American Magazine of Art*, April 1926, pp. 170–74.

"Modernist Furnishings in Paris." *Good Furniture Magazine*, May 1927, pp. 243–46.

Mumford, Lewis. "American Taste." *Harpers Monthly* 155 (Oct. 1927): 569–77.

———. "Culture and Machine Art." In *Annual of American Design 1931*. *See* Leonard and Glassgold, 1930.

Naylor, Blanch. "American Design Progress." *Design* 33 (Sept. 1931): 82–89.

Naylor, Gilian. *The Bauhaus*. London: Studio Vista, 1968.

"$19,900 Paid at Art Sale." *New York Times*, April 28, 1940.

"New Muse Leads Art Rebels Here." Unknown newspaper, Feb. 11, 1911. Clipping in Cleveland Institute of Art "Scrapbook," vol. 3, p. 55.

Nutting, Wallace. *Furniture Treasury*, vol. 1. New York: Macmillan, 1928.

Ostergard, Derek E. *Mackintosh to Mollino: Fifty Years of Chair Design*. New York: Barry Friedman, 1983.

Parke-Bernet Galleries. *Furniture and Decorations: Estate of the Late Louis Rorimer, April 25, 26, and 27, 1940*. New York: Parke-Bernet, 1940.

Pilgrim, Dianne. "Decorative Art: The Domestic Environment." In Brooklyn Museum, *The American Renaissance 1876–1917*. Brooklyn: Brooklyn Museum, 1979.

Pool, Ethel. "Louis Rorimer Finds New Art Note in Paris Exhibit." *Country Club News*, Aug. 25, 1925, pp. 33–34.

"Prepare the Way for Euclid-Av Hotel." *Cleveland Plain Dealer*, Oct. 26, 1910.

Pulos, Arthur. *American Design Ethic: A History of Industrial Design*. Cambridge: MIT Press, 1983.

Purdy, W. Frank. "The Taste of the American People." *Arts and Decoration*, Nov. 1920, pp. 38, 64, and 66.

Quick, Michael. *Munich and American Realism in the 19th Century*. Sacramento: Crocker Art Gallery, 1978.

Raley, Dorothy, ed. *A Century of Progress: Homes and Furnishings*. Chicago: M. A. Ring, 1934.

Reid, Kenneth. "Norman Bel Geddes, Master of Design." *Pencil Points*, Jan. 1937, pp. 1–32.

Richards, C. R. "Sane and Insane Modernism in Furniture." *Good Furniture Magazine,* Jan. 1929, pp. 8–14.

Robbins, Carle. "Cowan of Cleveland, Follower of an Ancient Craft." *Cleveland Bystander,* Sept. 7, 1929, pp. 10–13.

——— . "Louis Rorimer—Three Dimensional Man." *Cleveland Bystander* 11, no. 50 (Dec. 14, 1929): 31–35.

Rocky River Public Library. *Cowan Pottery Museum.* Rocky River, Ohio, 1978.

Rorimer, James J. *The Metropolitan Museum of Art: The Cloisters.* New York: The Metropolitan Museum of Art, 1939.

"Rorimer Sale Ends Today." *New York Times,* April 27, 1940.

Rose, William Ganson. *Cleveland: The Making of a City.* Cleveland: World, 1950.

Rosenthal, Rudolph, and Helena Ratzka. *The Story of Modern Applied Art.* New York: Harper and Bros., 1948.

Sanders, Barry, ed. *The Craftsman: An Anthology.* Salt Lake City: Peregrine Smith, 1978.

Sanford, Nellie C. "An Architect-Designer of Modern Furniture." *Good Furniture Magazine* 30, no. 3 (March 1928): 116–18.

——— . "Decorating in Art Moderne." *Good Furniture Magazine* 31, no. 5 (Nov. 1928): 241–45.

Scarlett, Frank, and Marjorie Townly. *Arts Decoratifs: A Personal Recollection of the 1925 Paris Exhibition.* London: Academy, 1975.

Schweiger, Werner. *Wiener Werkstaette: Design in Vienna 1903–1932.* New York: Abbeville, 1984.

Seale, William. *The Tasteful Interlude: American Interiors through the Camera's Eye 1860–1917.* 2d ed. Nashville: American Association for State and Local History, 1981.

Sheraton, Thomas. *The Cabinet-Maker and Upholsterer's Drawing Book.* 3d rev. ed. London: T. Bensley, 1802. Reprint. New York: Praeger, 1970.

Society of Arts and Crafts. *Handicraft,* vol. 1 and 2. Boston: Society of Arts and Crafts, 1902–3.

Solon, Leon V. "The Viennese Method for Artistic Display: New York Galleries of the Wiener Werkstaette of America." *Architectural Record,* March 1923, pp. 266–71.

"Splendid New Public Dining Rooms Opened in Statler Hotels of Cleveland and Detroit." *The Western Hotel and Restaurant Reporter* 62, no. 2 (February 1938): 8–10 and 22.

"Statler Chiefs at New Lounge Opening." *Hotel and Restaurant News,* Oct. 1, 1938, p. 2.

Stone, May N. "Hotel Pennsylvania: Strictly First-Class Accommodations at Affordable Rates" (master's thesis, Columbia University, 1988), pp. 67–70.

Tate, Allen, and C. Ray Smith. *Interior Design in the Twentieth Century.* New York: Harper and Row, 1986.

Taylor Chair Company. *The Taylor Chair Company: Seven Generations Since 1816.* Bedford, Ohio: Taylor Chair, 1982.

"Taylor-Horrocks Executive Suites, Authentic Period Designs." *Catalogue No. 122 Special Recorded Edition,* book no. 406. Bedford, Ohio: Taylor Chair [1930].

Thackrey, Helen. "A House and Garden in the Woods." *Your Garden* 3, no. 6 (Oct. 1929): 15 and 39.

Tomkins, Calvin. "The Cloisters . . . The Cloisters . . . The Cloisters." *Metropolitan Museum of Art Bulletin,* March 1970, pp. 316 and 320.

Townsend, Reginald. *The Book of Building and Interior Decoration.* Garden City, N.Y.: Doubleday, Page, 1923.

Triggs, Oscar Lovell. *Chapters in the History of the Arts and Crafts Movement.* Chicago, 1902. Reprint. New York: Arno, 1979.

United States Department of Commerce. *Report of the Commission Appointed by the Secretary of Commerce to Visit and Report upon the International Exposition of Modern Decorative and Industrial Art in Paris 1925.* Washington, D.C.: U.S. Commerce Department, 1926.

United States Department of Commerce, Bureau of Census. *Historical Statistics of the United States: Colonial Times to 1970.* Washington, D.C.: Commerce Department, 1975.

Van Alen, William. "The Structure and Metal Work of the Chrysler Building." *The Architectural Forum* 53, no. 4 (Oct. 1930): 494 and 497.

Veronesi, Giulia. *Style and Design 1909–1929.* New York: Brazillier, 1968.

Vincent, Sidney, and Judah Rubenstein. *Merging Traditions: Jewish Life in Cleveland.* Cleveland: WRHS and Jewish Community Federation of Cleveland, 1978.

Vollmer, William A., ed. *A Book of Distinctive Interiors.* New York: McBride, Nast, 1912.

Weber, Eva. *Art Deco in America.* New York: Simon and Schuster, 1985.

Wharton, Edith, and Ogden Codman, Jr. *The Decoration of Houses.* New York: Scribner's, 1902. Reprint. New York: W. W. Norton, 1978.

Wheeler, Candace. *Principles of Home Decoration.* Garden City, N.Y.: Doubleday, Page, 1903.

Whitford, Frank. *Bauhaus.* London: Thames and Hudson, 1985.

Whitney Museum of Art. *High Style: Twentieth Century American Design.* New York: Whitney Museum of Art, 1986.

Willson, Winifred. "Beautiful Antique and Modern House Furnishings." *Arts and Decoration,* Feb. 1925, pp. 48, 50, and 75.

Wixom, Nancy Coe. *Cleveland Institute of Art: The First Hundred Years 1882–1982.* Cleveland: Cleveland Institute of Art, 1983.

INDEX

145